D1553154

SILENCED BY PRAYER

Peter Ward C.Ss.R.

Silenced by Prayer
From Words to Contemplation

He sets a time for sorrow
and a time for joy.
A time for silence
And a time for talk.
Ecclesiastes 3:4,7

the columba press

First published in 1999 by
the columba press
55A Spruce Avenue, Stillorgan Industrial Park,
Blackrock, Co Dublin

Cover by Bill Bolger
Origination by The Columba Press
Printed in Ireland by Colour Books Ltd, Dublin

ISBN 1 85607 252 5

Contents

Abbreviations

St John of the Cross

AMC *The Ascent of Mount Carmel*
  vg: AMC 1, 9, 3 = *Ascent*, Bk 1, ch 9, par 3.
DN *The Dark Night*
  vg: DN 1, 14, 4 = *Dark Night*, Bk 1, ch 14, par 4.
CANT *The Spiritual Canticle*
  vg: Cant 14, 3 = *Canticle*, Stanza 14, par 3.
LF *The Living Flame of Love*
  vg: LF 2, 30 = *Living Flame*, Stanza 2, par 30.

St Teresa of Avila

Life *The Autobiography*
  vg: Life 11, 7. = *Life*, ch 11, par 7.
IC *The Interior Castle*
  vg: IC 5, 3, 3 = *Castle*, Mansion 5, ch.3, par 3.

Introductory Note

I was in my mid-thirties when I began to suspect that there had to be more than this to prayer. Surely it was not just about saying words to an absent God. That was when the search really started.

Then, gradually, the stages of prayer began to unfold until now I can look back on a journey with you, because I think it is the journey of everyone though the details and circumstances may be different.

But how did this journey first start? I am sure most of us do not remember. But I imagine it was somewhat like this, at least here in Catholic Ireland. When our parents were putting us to bed at night they probably told us to say our prayers. Since we did not know any prayers, they probably taught us simple prayers like: 'God bless daddy and mammy', God bless John and Mary', 'God make granny better'. Those little prayers were added to at home and later at school. Before long we had many prayers. The way our prayer developed after that depended on the circumstances of each family. It is that development I want to explore in this book.

I will base what I have to say on the masters of the spiritual life, on the experiences of others, and on my own experience. I will tell you how I think my own prayer developed, as it is the only story of prayer that I know well. This will give you a pattern with which to compare yours, either because your development is different from mine or because it is like it.

I see prayer usually developing through these stages: 1. The Prayer of Struggle. 2. The Prayer of Simplicity. 3. The Prayer of Contemplation. These will be the three main parts of the book.

Writing a book is a lonely affair. When I finished the first draft, I wondered how others would react to it. So I thank all those who helped me by reading the typescript and offering suggestions and encouragement. Especially do I want to thank Fr Eltin Griffin, O. Carm, and others who helped me in any way.

I am grateful to my superiors and confreres who gave me the freedom needed to write and who put up with me!

PART 1

First Stage of Prayer:
The Prayer of Struggle

CHAPTER 1

My Early Attempts at Prayer

When I was about seven years of age, my family came to live on the Falls Road in Belfast. There was my father and mother, my older brother and younger sister. My father ran a very successful off-licence. As we lived near Clonard Monastery, run by the Redemptorists, the family went to Mass there. Then my brother and I became altar boys. Most of my early recollections of prayer go back to those altar boy days. I think my idea of prayer was formed in Clonard and at home and in school, though, no doubt, Clonard was a big influence.

The Influence of Clonard
As altar boys we went to Mass every morning. If I remember rightly, I used serve the 7.45 Mass each morning. On some evenings of the week there were what we used call 'devotions'. These consisted of the rosary, followed by special prayers and ending with Benediction. Every Sunday evening we had a more solemn rosary, sermon and Benediction, which attracted a big crowd. Even bigger crowds came when there was a special course of sermons. I remember one course that was packed. The theme was 'Characters of the Reformation' with sermons, among others, on Henry VIII and Martin Luther. I still remember the crowds of well-known Catholics who came to the courses. I found all that exciting. As good as the pictures – well not quite! Could anything have been as good as the pictures? Then there was the Boys' Confraternity every Wednesday evening when the church was packed with primary school boys. The noise was deafening. Then the altar boys had a meeting every week. No doubt about it, Clonard played a big part in our lives. It was not that our family was holier than others. For a number of us boys, it was part of the routine.

How we prayed

I think the daily and Sunday Mass and the 'devotions' were our
school of prayer. They had the stamp of that period. When the people gathered in the church, there was a lot of activity, like reciting
prayers together, answering prayers read by a priest, listening to
sermons and singing. I am certain we boys were bored and did a lot
of talking and looking around during the Mass or Benediction. But
it was something to do, instead of sitting at home. There was no TV
at that time and we had no radio and did not get to the pictures all
that often. Besides, during these communal prayers we were rarely
left on our own. We were kept at the reciting or listening or singing.
You could say we were really being entertained and kept occupied
in God's presence. Nobody ever suggested we pray silently on our
own.

When there was silence, as during the old Latin Mass, most people said the rosary, read from their missals or prayer books, or just
day-dreamed or looked around. Perhaps we boys tried not to be too
fidgety and made sure not to be caught talking!

Our 'silent' prayer after communion was spent in saying or reading well known prayers. Prayer books had many 'Prayers during
Mass' and 'Prayers after Communion'. A great practice at the time
was getting through one's personal prayers. Many people carried
their little bundle of leaflets or novenas or memory cards of dead
relations and read through them. Indeed many people still do that.

The Family Rosary

Then at home the family said the rosary and litanies together, usually
with our heads stuck in a chair! That we hated because it was too
long. Then we said a few hurried personal prayers beside our bedside morning and night. These too were vocal prayers, like the three
Hail Mary's for purity and the prayer for a happy death. All these
we recited by rote.

Another form of prayer I learned in Clonard, and from the
example of my mother, was the Way of the Cross. The stations, as
we called them, played a big part in Redemptorist spirituality. I
remember often in the morning after serving the quarter to eight

Mass, before returning home for breakfast, going around the beautiful big stations on my own in Clonard. Though I do not remember
how I prayed when going around, I grew up conscious of the suffering and death of Christ.

When I came back from Mass each morning the fire was burning
merrily in the polished grate. I loved that time eating my breakfast
and reading about the Abyssinian war in the paper, before running
across the road to school.

Books were important at home

Education and books were important in our home. A lovely memory
I have is the three of us sitting around my mother in the front room
while she read to us. She read beautifully. My brother, who became
a voracious reader, later filled the house with books. One of our
teachers encouraged us to go to the public library, which was only a
few hundred yards from the school. I made friends in the library
and heard about books the other boys were reading.

My mother must have been a brave woman, because my father
died when I was ten years old. Though she was gentle, she had the
courage to continue the family business with the help of her brother.
I am eternally grateful to him and his wife. Though my mother herself had not gone beyond primary school, she wanted us to be edu-
cated. She used say constantly, 'Keep at the books. Keep at the
books.' And she put that into practice when we left primary school.
Even though we did not live very far from St Malachy's College,
she sent my brother and me as boarders. It was expensive but she
had the money and that was how she wanted to use it. Besides, she
thought I would not study well at home. She knew her son! I am so
grateful to her for her foresight.

Prayer in Boarding School

So boarding school it was for me at thirteen years of age, with my
big brother to make sure I studied. It was there I learned to look
after myself; there was no mammy to run to. Not long after I went
to St Malachy's, we had a retreat preached by a well known
Redemptorist, Fr Paddy Kelly. He spoke about vocations so I went

to see him and told him I wanted to be a priest. He asked me to call to see him in Clonard and, before I knew, it was arranged that I would go to our Redemptorist College in Limerick. After one year in St Malachy's I went there. Indeed, I spent all my secondary school years, from thirteen on, away from home as a boarder.

In boarding school, especially in Limerick, the pattern of prayer was not very different from at home. We had daily Mass. We went to the big church for the usual Sunday Mass. There was always a sermon and it was of a certain type. It was not the homily or the commentary on the scripture reading we get nowadays. In most dioceses the bishop drew up a list of instructions to be preached each Sunday. One year, the course would be on the Ten Commandments, another year it would be the precepts of the church, another the seven deadly sins and so on. They were truly instructions, teaching us our obligations. They taught us a lot about living the Christian life. And that was backed up by what we learned in catechism class.

Then on Sunday evenings there were 'devotions' just as in Clonard and these we attended. In our college chapel we had our own daily devotions like the rosary, visits to the Blessed Sacrament, prayers to Our Lady and St Joseph, the Way of the Cross.

These prayers were part of my life as a teenager. We were not in any way more pious than others, far from it. Most boys of the group I moved with were the same. Thanks be to God, we did not get into rowdyism or get involved in the IRA. How we escaped, I do not know. But I do remember being very homesick, especially after the Christmas holidays. One Christmas someone at home gave me a present of a little diary and I made short entries in it when I returned to school. Reading it later, I was surprised to discover that for more than a month I kept writing, 'I am still homesick', 'I hate being back at school'.

Then there were hours of study, difficult teachers, trembling going into some classes (one in particular), unattractive subjects, surviving with the other boys, misunderstandings and rows, getting into trouble with those in charge. I had my share of misunderstandings with the priest in charge. It is strange, with all the talk we have nowadays, I do not remember being bullied or sexually assaulted.

The Excitement of Growing up

But we were not saying our prayers in a vacuum. They were said against the backdrop of our home life and school life and above all our growing up. I was now into my teens and they tell us that is a time of crisis. We were, of course, becoming adults. We were developing physically and I was not bad at football and swimming and gym. I was tough for my size and age.

Intellectually we were beginning to ask questions. I remember I could not understand all the fuss about a book that was popular at that time. It was 'Gone with the Wind' by Margaret Mitchell. It was denounced from the pulpit and in the Catholic press. I read it when I was at home on holidays, as I could not bring it back to school because it was considered an 'immoral' book. The heroine was Scarlett O'Hara, a self-willed girl who led a bad life. I remember boldly proclaiming that the author was free to portray her heroine as she wanted, Catholic or not.

And, of course, the hormones were flowing through our veins. Girls were becoming interesting and exciting. I remember at school three of us got into trouble for talking about girls. Oh horror! When the priest in charge found out about this, he paraded us before the whole school and punished us very severely. And it really was severely. He continued the punishment in class by paying absolutely no attention to me even when I put up my hand to answer. And yet I survived it. He told me later that I stood up to the test very well. As a result, we became great friends in school and later. He was the first man I could comfortably go to with my problems.

During the holidays at home, I used meet many girls through my brother and his friends. I can still picture lovely summer evenings walking up the Falls Road with my brother to join the other boys and girls. And that glorious month we used spend in Portstewart every summer. I found some of the girls very attractive and fell for them. But it was all so innocent. And the strange thing was, in my last years, when I returned to school after the holidays, I told that same priest, who had given me such a battering, all about my romantic trysts. This time he did not threaten to send me away! I suppose it was healthier to talk about this very human attraction.

I loved the holidays and found them quite thrilling. They gave me a sense of excitement and freedom. Yes, at times, life was worth living. Strange how we always remember the sunny days! Did it ever rain during those holidays?

And so there were many different layers in my life, as in that of every teenager. There was the life of study and reading. There was life with the other boys and the teachers, mostly Redemptorists. There was the excitement of the holidays with the pictures and swimming and the discovery of girls. And then there was life with my family during holidays and by letter.

Following our Peers

There I was, as mixed up as any teenager in that time of crisis and upheaval. They tell us the influence of the parents and of those in authority begins to fade in the teens and the influence of the peer group becomes stronger. That was the same with us. We too thought that our elders were out of date and old fogies who did not know what was going on. Just like teenagers in ever generation, we too followed the peer group in songs and films and dress. We too would have liked to be more free to go with whoever we wanted and where we wanted. But we did not voice our dissent, we just tried to get away with it! There was none of that open rebellion against authority we have witnessed since the 60s. Nor was there a throwing away of moral standards, though we thought some of the rules were too rigid. In those days the few who did speak out were considered cranks and often censored. Great writers like Frank O'Connor and Edna O'Brien. Somehow, I never got into that conservative way of thinking, even later. But I kept my opinions to myself. Was that cowardice or prudence?

Our Attitude to the Church

However, we held priests in great respect. As for the church, we were all for it! It was the time of public display and of processions in honour of the Sacred Heart and Our Lady. One banner, proudly held aloft in processions in Belfast, proclaimed, with great affection though bad theology, 'God bless the Sacred Heart'! Now we see that the church, though persecuted in many ways, was really triumphalistic. After all it was the holy, catholic and apostolic church! We followed the party line and thought we were superior to other religions. And, of course, there were people we had to beware of. Those Protestants were, after all, heretics! Further afield, there were pagans and infidels whom perhaps we would never meet. But the worst of all were the communists. They were the enemies who persecuted the church and were out to destroy it. The Pope, the bishops and many writers condemned Lenin and Trotsky and Stalin. All that we would oppose like good Catholics. I now smile at how sectarian we were.

And all the while our teens were passing. We went back to school. We studied and went to class and played games. And each day we went to Mass and said our prayers and had our devotions. But how far was God really in our lives and how far did our prayers really express a relationship with God?

CHAPTER 2

How Aware of God were we?

That was the way we lived our Catholic lives and that was the external form of our prayer. It is easy enough to describe the externals – the words we used, the kind of prayers we said, the sermons we heard, the rites of the sacraments, the devotions we attended. But that is not really what prayer is about. Words and formulas and rites could be mere words or mumbo jumbo. There must be another element and that, of course, is God. The catechism defines prayer as raising the mind to God. But in our words and rites how aware of God were we and what did God mean to us?

At this distance in time it would be almost impossible to recreate my awareness of God. But there are indications that may be pointers. Indications that God was stirring in me.

Our attitude to God
We all knew about God because we were constantly hearing about him. We were told to pray to him; he was mentioned in sermons and catechism was about him. I think I had some kind of an awareness of him, that he was about somewhere or other, though far away and up there somewhere. I had no sense of presence as of one near me or touching me. Even that threatening painting of the all-seeing eye of God did not frighten me. And yet he did impinge on my life. I knew in some way that it was to him I was praying. I had a sense of sin, but it lay lightly on my shoulders. I never had any fear of punishment coming from him. Thank God I was never scrupulous. Yet I never thought of him as someone I should have a personal relationship with. It was more a matter of doing the things he told us to do, reciting prayers and going to Mass and giving up sweets during Lent and doing what my parents wanted and not stealing or telling lies.

And then they were always talking about the 'soul' and we were told to 'save our souls'. Yet, when I was very young I had great difficulty in trying to understand what 'the soul' was. It was only later I discovered that my soul is the inner part of me that I cannot see but which really makes me tick. It is the life source within me that will continue to live when my body dies.

Was God stirring in me?
One thing I loved to do in my teens, when I was at home, was to go and sit in the front room alone. I wonder if it had anything to do with prayer. When I was in the mood, I could go into a kind of reverie, quite contented to sit there in silence for hours. I would try to puzzle out questions that were annoying me. I wondered who God was and what he was like. Another big mystery was what was eternity like? I used to try to imagine life going on and on and on. When I concentrated on that it made me dizzy.

Was this in any way connected with awareness of God? I ask that because of still another experience I had which stirred me profoundly. It was the death of my father when I was ten years of age.

A shattering Blow
When we were very young we used spend our summer holidays in my mother's old home in Inniskeen, Co Monaghan. It was a very small farm. There was not a lot of money around and few of the amenities of the city. But we loved it because we had plenty of the basic simple things of life and were as free as the birds for a couple of weeks. That particular summer my mother came to bring us home for the opening of school. We arrived back in Belfast and that night we were allowed to wait up until my father came back home from the shop. He came in as happy and joyful as ever, obviously pleased that the three of us were back. He hugged us and tossed us up in the air. And off we went to bed, no doubt very tired but happy.

When I got up in the morning I came down to get my breakfast and face into school again. I remember saying, 'I hate going back to school.' An aunt of mine, who was there, said, 'You are not going to school today.' When I asked why she said, 'Your daddy is dead.'

During the night my father became ill. Though I did not know it at the time, he had a heart condition. My mother sent for the doctor and the priest. But all to no avail. He died during the night, of a heart attack. She did not disturb my brother or sister or me. We slept on. So it was the next morning I first heard of it.

I was dumbfounded. I did not quite know what death meant. I had seen dead people, but they were all neighbours or strangers. No one in the family or among my relations had died. But I did realise that something terrible had happened. My daddy had gone and I knew he would not come back. A kind of numbness descended on me. I seemed to be in another world. Then I began to wonder where the body was. I was afraid to see it and terrified lest I would. Was it in my parents' bedroom? Or was it in the front room down stairs? I did not want to stumble on it by accident. I escaped to my bedroom. There I was safe. I remember meeting my mother on the landing outside the bedroom where I discovered the body was. She was in a terrible state, crying and I had never seen her crying like that before. She put her arms around me and then she took me by the hand to lead me into the bedroom to see my father's body. But I could not face it. I pulled back and said 'No. No.' She gently tried to persuade me, but I kept saying 'No.' Then she let me go and I ran down the stairs.

I did eventually venture into the room. By that time the family relations had come. There were chairs along the walls of the room and through the open bedroom door I could see my grandmother and others sitting there praying or talking. It was the sight of my grandmother looking so calm that gave me the courage. I ventured into the room and saw my father's body dressed in a brown shroud lying on the bed. There was the usual white bed linen. On a small bedside table, there were wax candles and a big silver crucifix. My father's face and hands looked waxen, like marble. Someone lead me to the body and put my hand on his forehead. It was the first time I ever touched a corpse. He was icy cold. The transformation astonished me. But at last I had faced up to it, at least to seeing my father's body. After that I went in and out of the room freely.

But the dreadful numbness lingered on. I struggled to find out

what this thing called death meant. I could not believe my daddy
was gone. As the days went by, when there was a ring at the front
door I would not have been surprised if he had walked in. One little
incident sticks in my mind. Some time later I went to Clonard to
serve Mass as usual. It was probably the 7.45. I was dressed in
black. I must have been very silent because another altar boy said to
me, 'What's wrong?' I said to him, 'My father has died.' And I went
back to school and still the thought of his death stayed with me.

In a Daze
Eventually, life got back to normal, though not quite. I went around
in a daze, like in a dream. I served Mass in Clonard, I went across
the road to school. Every Sunday afternoon after dinner, my mother
and the three of us went up to Milltown cemetery to visit the grave.
But that sense of gloom and loss used hit me frequently. And I think
it went on for some time, for weeks anyway, if not for months. It
was as if everything had completely changed. I began to realise that
life in the family was not as permanent as I had taken for granted.
After all, my father had just disappeared from our family. This was
an aspect of life I suddenly came face to face with. I knew then that
things did not just go on as usual for ever. Yet there seemed to be no
explanation. The sense of loss and emptiness that followed was
something new, outside the ordinary. So it seemed possible that
there would be other shocks awaiting me in life.

I do not want to read too much into my boyhood reactions, but I
wonder was it then that I first sensed that the 'beyond' was a possibility. Was I beginning to realise that there was something more
than what we can see and hear and touch around us? Was there
another world? I had heard of death and heaven and hell before.
But now it came into our family. As a result it was more real.
Everyone kept assuring me that Daddy had gone to heaven, or it
may have been purgatory. In any case into another life. I suppose I
was really groping with the meaning of life and death.

By the way do not imagine that children of ten do not feel deeply.
I am sure there are many like me. At ten I could not understand
death, but I felt it. Apart from the theology of it all, I have been seeking for ways to explain what I went through mentally and emotionally.

However, down the years some films and books and plays and deaths have had the same effect on me. Whether I am more susceptible to these things than others I do not know. But another incident happened some years later while I was still young.

Love on the Dole

I was 16 years of age and I was going back to school in Limerick on my own. I had a few hours in Dublin and went to a film. It was one that was talked about a lot at the time, 'Love on the Dole'. It was the story of a family that fell on hard times and descended into poverty. It terrified me. In our family we had never experienced poverty. Though we were not rich we had enough and more than many. But here was the story of how poverty drags a family down. I remember thinking how terrible it would be if my family and I were to descend into grinding poverty like that. I left the picture house feeling how degrading it would be. I realised how almost impossible it was to rise out of such poverty. A feeling of dread took me over. I remember I wrote that story in an essay for the English class. It was one of the few times I got 'good'!

My reaction to my father's death and to 'Love on the Dole', seem to have had something in common. There was the same sensation of being stunned and saddened and being taken out of myself. They were all of a piece. Was this, really, being brought to a new depth? Was I facing a deep, universal, aspect of life, which was so big I could not grasp it but only stand helpless before it?

In recent years I have been wondering if all these events are another aspect of deep prayer? They opened me up to something beyond daily life. Indeed, they went beyond the verbal. They said something I sensed in my feelings and emotions and could not put into words. When we are brought into this other world, are these deep insights, glimpses of the beyond, of the transcendent, of God?

Though it was to be some years before I experienced anything like that again, my father's death and even 'Love on the Dole', still stand out as landmarks. But there were still other things that were more directly religious and connected with prayer.

A certain awareness of Christ

During my school days, I was aware of Christ, though with less intensity. Through sermons and catechism I was aware of his life and teaching. Because of the Redemptorist emphasis in Clonard and in Limerick on the Way of the Cross, I was especially conscious of Christ's suffering and death. Some people may not realise it but at that time, I am talking of the 1940s, the resurrection was not a living part of our theology. We became aware of its real significance only in the 1960s. But his passion and death played a big part in our early lives. I remember one Good Friday afternoon while I was still in primary school, asking my mother, when I was with her in the shop, what time it was. She said, 'It is almost three. Why?' I said, 'That is the time Our Lord died.'

The Passion in Holy Week

However, it was in boarding school in Limerick that Holy Week became very special to me. We did not get home for holidays at Easter. And so we had a retreat during the last three days of Holy Week. That I loved. Indeed, I loved the retreats in general, both the Easter and summer ones. One reason was that it was the only occasion we had free time and were not herded around together! We were free to go to the study hall or the chapel or the garden to read or pray. I remember sitting in the garden in pleasant Easter weather, reading. It was a delight. Then we went to the church each evening for Tenebrae, the evening office of the church which has fallen out completely as public prayer. As we were connected with the Redemptorists by being in the Juvenate, we wore our surplices and soutanes and sat up on the sanctuary with the Fathers and Brothers. I suppose that made us feel special and part of the establishment! The evening office was read in Latin and we had our books. I loved trying to keep up with the reading of the Latin, but the priests were too fast for us. However, that was our first taste of the Breviary.

But the most delightful memory of the retreat was something that may surprise others. It was the reading in the refectory at meals during the three days of retreat. The custom was to read one of those 'Lives of Christ' like the ones by the Abbè Fouard or

Archbishop Goodier. The chapters on the passion and death of Christ were picked out. They were a marvellous explanation of what the gospel story was about. It is true they might seem very out of date nowadays, but they made the gospels become alive for me. I loved listening to the charming details of life at that time in Palestine. Then we were told who the scribes and pharisees were and why they wanted Jesus put to death. We heard all the little details of the trial and the crucifixion of Jesus. These books pointed out the difference between each of the gospel accounts. They spoke of the characters of the people involved. I remember I listened enthralled. It was the first time I was really interested in the gospels. It was a taste of what scripture study could be like.

What kind of prayer was this?

That was the way we prayed right through primary and secondary school. We said our prayers at home and in church, we went to Mass, we made retreats. But what kind of prayer was it? Were we ever urged to have a personal relationship with God or Christ?

Our prayer was mostly vocal prayer: we used the prayers we learned as children; we read our missals at Mass; we had prayer books for other occasions. We joined in the rosary and the litanies. And it was usually prayer of petition. We prayed for things we wanted. We prayed for others.

And yet, there were those glimpses of something more, like my being stunned after father's death and the film, 'Love on the Dole'. But it was only in later years that I began to see some significance in them. And so I will try to explore that in later chapters.

I wonder how young people pray today? I imagine it would be more or less the same. However, they have great advantages like retreats that get them talking personally, and Taize chants and praying before a lighted candle and with incense. These external things do create an atmosphere. But, do young people have deeper stirrings within themselves? They must do, though they may not be able to articulate it. I couldn't at their age. I would be interested to hear what they have to say.

But a new element was about to come into my prayer.

CHAPTER 3

A New kind of Prayer – Meditation

I remember that dread day in August 1944, when Sean Bennett and I said goodbye to our families at the station in Belfast. Then we walked along the platform and, without looking back, manfully got on to the train! We were off to the novitiate in Dundalk. In other words we were 'leaving the world' and had just said farewell to our parents and brothers and sisters. A symbol of what we were leaving behind was that we smoked our last cigarettes on the journey and gave those left over to a porter at Dundalk station, much to his delight! It was years before I smoked a cigarette again. But at that moment, I felt it was 'Never more Miranda! Never more'. That was the image of religious life at that time. We were giving up the world. And the fleshpots of Belfast, whatever they were, would never be ours.

Monastic Prayer
When we reached Dundalk, we were thrown into monastic life at the deep end. After a sleep until 7.30 for a few mornings, we had to follow the rigorous routine of novitiate life. We got up at 5.30 each morning. There was silence most of the day. We had three half hours of meditation a day, besides the many other community prayers. We had conferences of which we had to take notes. Manual work was a big part of our routine, both in the house and in the garden. We were forbidden contact with outsiders and even with the rest of the community. Penances and correction were the order of the day. But there was no starvation. Indeed, there was plenty to eat. And yet we were happy enough, except when the Novice Master corrected us and that happened frequently. Looking back on it now, I realise that human beings can get used to almost any

regime! I have seen prisoners settling down to life in Long Kesh and
Crumlin Road jail. Early rising or a full timetable or strict penances
are not the most difficult things in life.

A new type of prayer

I soon began to discover that prayer in the novitiate was a mixture.
The form of prayer I followed at home, in Clonard and in boarding
school, continued. We had Mass, devotions, novenas, rosary and, of
course, the usual sermon and benediction in the church on Sunday
evening. There were long periods of vocal prayers. Nothing very
different about that. However, there was a new element. We were
introduced to meditation.

I remember my surprise at the beginning when told there were
three half hours of prayer each day. Morning and evening, we went
along with the whole community to the oratory. After some intro-
ductory prayers, one of the novices stood up and read a short passage from a meditation book. The light was put out and there we
were in darkness and in silence. And that lasted for half an hour. It
was completely different from any prayer I had done before. I wondered what in the name of heavens we were supposed to do during
that half hour. Well, whatever it was, we had to do it three times a
day because we novices had an extra half hour alone in our rooms
in the afternoon. Then, at least, because I was alone, I could move
around the room and look out the window!

Then one day the Novice Master gave us a talk on meditation. It
was the first of many talks on the subject. The general idea was this:

The first part of meditation

Our Novice Master told us there were two parts in the meditation.
When the passage was read the first thing we had to do was reflect
on the meaning of what we heard. We had to ask ourselves what
exactly the passage meant and spend some time analysing it. Then
we had to ask how this applied to our lives. Where did we fail in
this virtue or how were we not following the gospel? What was
God asking us to do about it? The plan was, read, analyse and apply
to our lives.

This first part was known as *discursive prayer*. Discursive comes from the latin word *currere,* to run. Here it means running from idea to idea in the mind, reasoning about the text. It was in this part of meditation we were to get new ideas and insights. This was the way we were to learn about God and the virtues and the gospels. These new insights we applied to our own lives.

Affective Prayer

The second part of the meditation was called *affective prayer.* This was the time for expressing our affection for God and Christ. It was the time for talking directly to them and telling them we loved them or that we wanted to love them. Of course, our love or our affection should have flowed spontaneously from the reflections we had just made. However, since this love might not flow we were urged to spend the time in making many affections or little acts. It was recommended that we make many acts of sorrow, trust, thanksgiving and above all of love. For example we could say, 'My God, I am sorry for offending you', or 'My God I trust in you', 'My God I want to love you'. This is why it is called affective prayer since here we tried to express our love and affection. This was the more important part of the meditation because here the real communion with God was to take place. Indeed it was the whole point of meditation, to be more closely united with God. Now, that was the basic theory of meditation.

Another part of the theory was that there should be an advance in our meditation. The advance should take place in a definite way. When we were first introduced to meditation it was accepted that we would, at the beginning, have to spend a lot of time at the discursive part. After all, at the start of our religious life, we did not know much about God or the gospels or the virtues. So we had to reflect a great deal on them. Eventually this knowledge would grow until it would not be necessary to spend so much time at the discursive part.

Then as we advanced, more and more time should be given to the second part, affective prayer. Eventually, this talking to God and making affections should occupy the greater part of the half hour. After all, that was what meditation was really about. Ultimately, little time would be spent on the discursive part. Then we were to end the meditation with resolutions to be carried out that day. That was the theory and it was logical.

And yet we failed

There were many reasons why we failed. The first was the difficulty of concentrating. We soon learned how difficult that was. In the silence of meditation it was even more difficult than at vocal prayer. I remember my thoughts would fly off in all directions. I daydreamed about home, about my work, or the misunderstandings I had with others, or about the telling off I expected to get from the Novice Master. I relived some incident from the past. I spent hours fantasising about the future. I am sure there was a lot of sexual fantasy. It was like King Claudius in Hamlet: 'My words rise up; my thoughts remain below.' My empty words went up to God, but not my thoughts! At confession I accused myself of giving into distractions at prayer.

But the greater failure was in the affective part. For most of us the affective part never really got going. It was only years later that I got some idea why we failed. The reason was simple. We had yet no idea of what love was. True we might have experienced some puppy love towards some of the girls we met. But as for love of God and affection for him that was beyond us! Indeed, it would take many years for us to make sense of that. And until such time that we began to get some little feeling of the love of God, the affective part of prayer would be artificial. Since nothing artificial can be entered into with enthusiasm I did not keep it up for long.

Yet a giant step forward

Most of us thought meditation was very difficult. I know that because, as novices, we used often tell each other of our failure. I remember only one fellow-novice who said he found it very easy. He did not last too long!

However, being introduced to meditation was a landmark. It was a new type of prayer, this thinking about God and talking to him personally. And, even more so, trying to love God personally was something we had never really been told about before. This led us into a new kind of prayer that lifted our communication with God above the recitation of vocal prayer. It was an attempt to get us personally involved with God. And so, I sensed that this was an important step. And, in fact, it did turn out to become the basis of the deeper prayer that usually follows. It now seems obvious to me that if we could have generated real affection for God in our meditations, we would have been led into deeper prayer very soon. However, that affection did not come and so I struggled for years. No doubt, there may have times when the meditation went well enough and I hit the jackpot. Perhaps during long retreats some passage of scripture opened up before me and I saw a new and deeper meaning in it. And this was always a thrill. But that was rare enough. And then it was back to the daily struggle. Many older religious tell me they had the same experience of failure.

And yet it was crucial for us to be introduced to meditation at this stage. It was to be the training ground for deeper prayer. Just as the mathematician had to start off with addition and subtraction and the musician had to spend boring hours practising scales, so we had to spend boring hours practising meditation.

It was only years later I could see another difficulty – we were trying to pray on our own. It was a man-centred exercise. We thought if we tried hard enough and kept at it long enough we would get there. Unfortunately, no one had told us about the Holy Spirit and how he leads us into prayer. Of course, the Spirit had not yet arrived! That was back in the 1940s.

The Novitiate ends

The novitiate was meant to help us come to know ourselves and to grow to know God through prayer. So we had many talks from the Novice Master and spent most of our time praying and at spiritual reading. We tried to overcome our faults, at least the external ones the Novice Master pointed out to us. Of course we had not really come to understand what our real deep faults were. That was another day's work, or should I say the work of years and years, at

least as far as I was concerned. No doubt in the novitiate we did try
to advance in prayer because we were in a hothouse atmosphere
with little outside distraction. And so at the end of the year we
probably felt we were deep into prayer and about to become the
greatest Redemptorists since St Alphonsus. Little did we know what
lay ahead!

CHAPTER 4

The New World of the Seminary

And then we found ourselves in the Seminary. In our house in Galway, Cluain Mhuire, where I was a student, there were about sixty young men, not counting the teaching staff and the professed community. The numbers were later to go up to 100. We were all in our late teens and early twenties. All healthy young men, full of energy. There were similar groups in seminaries all over the country. We were supposed to be there seeking God and preparing for the priesthood. Prayer was part of the holy work we were engaged in.

We had left the novitiate full of idealism. But that began to fade. For a little while we were shocked at how careless the older students had become about prayer and the rule. Imagine, I even saw students fighting – real fisty cuffs – on the football field!

A different world
So we raw novices landed in a different world. After the confined life in the novitiate, we were given freedom for new pursuits. Very soon our activities became engrossing and some were even exciting. Studies would, of course, be our main work for the next nine years. Like most of my particular year, I was appointed to go to the university and a new range of subjects opened up before us. Gradually our studies became our preoccupation. And, of course, there was the beautiful city of Galway to explore. I loved Galway from the beginning.

Besides, there were other things to involve us. There was reading and though the choice of books was restricted, it was wide enough to be interesting. We now had games a few times in the week and that could be exciting. For my size I was agile and good at football. In the summer there was swimming in Galway Bay and I was one of the enthusiasts. And on top of that, we had bits and pieces of work around the house and in the garden. Each student seemed to drift towards what attracted him. Some expressed themselves in gardening or bee-keeping or book binding. I got involved in printing. I suppose we were searching for ways to express our new found intellectual and artistic talents and our physical prowess. After some time I was invited into the drama group and the big Christmas play became one of my great interests.

But all this external activity was only one side of the story.

The subterranean waters
There are underground currents that began in our infancy. They are still bubbling away, and will be all our lives. It was true we had entered adolescence many years before, but we were still growing physically, intellectually, sexually and emotionally. Though we were scarcely aware of it, it was this development that preoccupied us and was the background music to all our other activities. Well, at least, it preoccupied me. I was becoming a new person. I wondered who I was and what kind of character I had and how I appeared to others. I tried to discover my strengths. I dreaded to find weaknesses in myself and would have hated to admit them. And often I came to know those weaknesses in a painful way, perhaps from the remarks of my companions, or corrections from my superiors. So this coming to terms with myself was bubbling away in my subconscious.

Our sexual development
Though it was never talked about openly the whole sexual development, too, was blossoming within us! We had to make our own way through that quagmire. But in the seminary there was no outlet for it, as we had little opportunity of coming in contact with girls. That would have been the natural thing at that age. Even at the university we were forbidden to talk to them. So they remained a big mystery and a mighty attraction. But the priest who had given me such a hard time in Limerick and later became a good friend of mine was now in charge of us. I found I could go to him and discuss my problems. That was a great safety valve. And even in our all male com-

munity I was not aware of homosexuality, so innocent was I. It, too, was not discussed. How we came out of that period as comparatively sane as we did, could well be discussed by psychologists! Perhaps it was due to the social life we had.

No doubt about it, there was great camaraderie and fun and joy. It was like the enclosed life of a village, with different aspects of human activity flourishing. And though life and the studies were difficult, they could be exciting. There was hope and so much to look forward to. With our new found strengths, the future was full of possibilities. I remember, when cycling to the university in Galway on spring mornings, quoting Wordsworth, 'Bliss was it in that dawn to be alive, but to be young was very heaven'. That youthful energy was coursing through our veins.

The struggle to pray

And it was with all these urges and energies and needs that prayer had to contend. At least for me it was a big struggle. I know that other students handled it better. So what chance did prayer have? My daily preoccupations were like the mad rush of a torrent of water from a broken dam. Everything was swept before it. And the delicate plant of prayer, nourished in the quiet of the novitiate, was sorely tested.

I remember one retreat I made when I was a student in Galway. Something the preacher said made me realise that I was becoming careless. So I plucked up my courage and went to him. I told him I was not praying well enough and had even lost my former interest in prayer and trying to become better. Other things, like my studies and games and plays, were more important in my life. When I had finished my story, he looked bewildered as if he did not know what to say. He seemed to be thinking, 'How could you become as lukewarm as that!' It was as if I had really gone to the dogs! Now, I thought, in all humility, that I had gone low, but wait a minute, not really as bad as that! I do not know if that reaction of the Retreat Master shook me up or led to a moment of conversion. If it did I do not remember!

The regrettable thing was that I really wanted to be good at prayer. I do not mean that I had dropped prayer altogether. There was no chance of that as we each had our own individual place in the chapel! God help us if we did not turn up at prayer time. We had to be there for the two half hours of meditation each day. Besides, we had our visits to the Blessed Sacrament and our Way of the Cross and the rosary and so forth. I myself added a few little bits and pieces here and there. Then there were retreats, every month and every year. Of course there were moments of crisis when I knew I needed prayer. And then I tried. But when those peak moments of retreat and crisis were over I was back to the daily round of 'real life'! That was back to my deep psychological needs and study and drama and games, and so there was no real urgency to my prayer.

Without that strict timetable of the seminary, I would have prayed even less. Indeed, at one time I thought that the important thing for us was English literature. I remember reading the 'Book of Job', not out of piety, but because someone pointed out it was a fine example of literature. I had certainly fallen from my ideals.

The tug of war

I think that for those who were as human as I am, there was a tug of war going on. On the one hand there was the desire to come closer to God. On the other hand there were many interesting pursuits enticing me away from prayer. But even more so, I was maturing and all the natural impulses I have enumerated were bubbling away within me. It could be described as a struggle between getting to know God and getting to know myself. Which was more impor- tant? No doubt they were equally important. That I know now. However, my own experience also leaves me in no doubt about which was the stronger pull at the time. The pull of nature is one of the deepest forces within us. It is irresistible and powerful. My weak resolutions to seek God and pray were no match for my raw human drives which were quite obsessive and compulsive. They were going to get their way, try as I might.

In the meantime I just struggled on from retreat to retreat. And as one resolution after another was broken, I realised more and more how weak I was. However, though this went on for years, it did not get me down. Hope springs eternal among young people.

A marvellous change

But then something unexpected happened. After six glorious years in Galway my superior told me I was going to India, with Gerry Morgan and Andy McGahey. He did not ask me if I wanted to go. I was told I was going! I was stunned when I heard the news but absolutely thrilled. I knew, of course, that leaving my family and my companions in Galway would be hard. But India was the one country in the world I wanted to go to. I suppose that was partly because of my schoolboy reading about the mysterious East and partly because of what returned missioners told us. It turned out to be one of the great adventures of my life. I will never forget the day the ship landed in Bombay. I gazed in amazement at sights and heard sounds and smelled smells that I would live with for years. It is an intriguing country, full of the unusual and unexpected. And Indians are lovely people to live with. I was enthralled from the beginning and wanted to see more.

Eventually we arrived at the seminary in Bangalore where many things were different and thrilling. Even on a walk in the city of Bangalore we met the most unusual things. Like the day we turned a corner to see six men carrying an upright piano on their heads. The lifestyle, of course, was radically different. The daily food was curry and rice which took months to get used to, though it is now one of my favourite dishes. We wore white cotton habits because of the heat. The dress of the people was exotic. And the languages! There are so many that Indians joke that the tower of Babel must have been built in India.

I had still three more years of my studies to do. Straightaway we were back to the routine of seminary life which was not all that different from Galway. There was the daily round of study and classes and games and recreation and prayer. Then we had to get to know our new companions. They say the Irish and Indians get on well together and we three seemed to fit in easily enough. And of course I had the same battle with prayer as in Galway. I remember those

hot and sticky morning and evening meditations when, in my day
dreaming, I was probably back in Galway or Belfast again.

New prayers, new work
Two years after I arrived I was ordained in our new church in
Bangalore. Even then I had another year of studies to do before I
was let loose on the vast sub-continent of India!

As priests there was a change in our pattern of prayer. We had to
say Mass every day and that has ever since been one of the high-
lights of my day. Then we had the obligation of the Divine Office,
comprised mostly of the psalms. Unfortunately, the emphasis
towards the breviary at that time was that every word was to be
said clearly and distinctly. So the attitude was to 'get it in', all the
words and before midnight! How we got it in and with what fervour seemed to be only of secondary importance.

As Redemptorist priests the first thing we had to prepare for
was preaching. It started with preaching a Sunday homily. Then we
had to write a series of mission sermons. As the years went by we
had to preach school retreats and parish missions and eventually
retreats to religious and priests. At times I was involved in parish
work. We had also to learn an Indian language. I was assigned to
Tamil and eventually went out on some Tamil missions. I found
that tough because I was not good at Tamil nor, indeed, at any foreign language. I have not the gift of tongues.

But the usual work throughout the year was the parish missions.
And the going could be hectic. When out on a parish mission we
had to preach morning and evening. During the day we tramped
the sun-baked streets of Bombay or wherever we were, visiting the
houses and the chawls and the slums. The rest of the time was taken
up with hearing confessions often till midnight. Usually we heard
hundreds of them. Then up again about five the next morning.
During Lent that usually went on for five or six consecutive weeks,
after which we were ready to drop. And yet I loved it, even the
tiredness. I found the bustle and excitement, especially of the big
city missions, exhilarating.

Soon I grew used to all these different kinds of work and loved the freedom of working in such a vast country. I often marvel at the daring all of us showed. Eventually I travelled all over India, usually in trains and frequently on my own. Especially in the north of India, I was often a lone European, without a word of the local languages and not a Christian in sight. Yet I loved the strangeness of everything around me. I always found it exciting going to parts of the country I had never visited before.

I give these details of my work because it was against the background of these activities that my prayer, such as it was, had to continue.

What happened to my prayer?

As a student in Bangalore there was the same struggle as in Galway with studies and prayer and work and getting to know myself. The combat continued because distractions are the same in every part of the world. But soon I was to leave the comparative shelter of the seminary life.

It was a different situation when I began my work as a missioner. Like my other companions I was constantly away from the monastery on missions and retreats. Then my prayer took a terrible battering. My life was go, go, all the time. Often I thought I was too busy to pray, even at home in the monastery. And yet I had time for reading and study and going to the pictures. On missions our personal prayer was left to ourselves and as a result I did not pray often enough. And when I did, you can image how badly it was done with worrying about my sermons and personal preoccupations.

Burdened with vocal prayer

But another situation militated against our getting more interested in prayer. Like most religious orders at that time, we were burdened with vocal prayer. Our morning and night prayer was a series of vocal prayers which we recited by heart. We had Mass every day and the daily rosary and visits to the Blessed Sacrament. There were the customary devotions and the Sunday night rosary, sermon and benediction. These were not very different from the time I was an altar boy. All these were vocal prayers. Then there were many vocal prayers which had to be recited privately.

One of our superiors in Galway made me realise how ridiculous our attitudes to prayer was. He was far ahead of his time. He mocked us for rushing around the oratory in one direction making the Way of the Cross, and in the other direction making the Way of the Divine Infant, a Redemptorist devotion. Then many of the students would walk along the corridor on the way to class, books in one hand, manual in the other, 'getting in' the penitential psalms, which were recommended. Much of our praying boiled down to words, words, words to be said and 'got in'. Personal affection for God and Jesus was not stressed. And yet there were many helpful traditions.

Helpful practices

These are some of the practices I found helpful. One was the visits to the Blessed Sacrament by St Alphonsus. They introduced me to a man who obviously loved God and spoke to him in sincere words of affection. Above all, the visits gave me a new vocabulary which could be used in prayer. St Alphonsus said things like, 'Grant that I may love you always and then do with me what thou wilt', 'I love you with my whole heart and give myself entirely to you. I ask for nothing more.' Even today these sentences keep running around in my mind. They were an example of what we were supposed to be doing at meditation which is expressing our affection for God. And, something I discovered later, they catch the spirit of the 'nada', the 'nothing', of St John of the Cross.

Another practice I loved was retreats. When we were in the seminary we had the annual six-day retreat. Generally, I threw myself into it and that helped revive my fervour. Two things were always stressed and they stirred my conscience. The first was prayer. I was usually shocked to discover I had failed again for another year. If it were not for this annual check-up, I might have been even worse, if that were possible. And then the retreat preacher always stressed fraternal charity, which I now see as one of the hardest parts of the religious life. There was always someone we did not see eye to eye with. An occurrence that seemed to happen every year, comes to my mind. We celebrated the last three days of Holy Week with great solemnity. That was before the new rite came in, so on Holy Thursday, we had the ceremony of the washing of the feet at mid-morning in the refectory. The Rector washed the feet of twelve confreres, the great sign of service and love, followed by a moving sermon on love of our brothers.

I often found myself saying, 'I am going to love all my confreres! After all, they're nice guys.' I am sure I meant that. Now, that was Thursday, but by Good Friday or Holy Saturday or certainly by Easter Sunday, I would be ready to throttle some of them! Charity and forgiveness still remain a battle for us mortals.

Unfortunately, those preached retreats ended when we left the seminary. As priests we had to make our annual retreat privately. I often longed to have a preached retreat. At one time our private retreat was for eight days, made in our own house and in our own room. I think I used take it seriously. And sometimes I could rouse up some fervour. But then when I returned to missions and retreats, it was back to struggling at prayer.

Thus the years passed. I was now in my mid-thirties and becoming a seasoned missioner, in the sense that I was quite used to the work. But the disappointing thing was that I had made little advance in prayer. It was still fundamentally the same as right back to when I was a seminarian in Galway and in Bangalore and as a young priest. I am astonished to think that there had been so little progress. It was still a mixture of vocal prayer and meditation.

And yet every now and again there were flashes of something deeper in my life. Perhaps they were the things that kept me going.

CHAPTER 5

Intimations of God in the Wilderness

When giving directed retreats I usually ask the retreatants, on the first night, to spend some time looking back on their lives. I suggest that they pick out the peak experiences, both the highs and the lows; the things that were joyful and the things that were painful. Many tell me that once they get started, they spend hours reviewing the past. They not only find it intriguing but are surprised at the things that come back to their minds. They rediscover incidents they had forgotten or paid little attention to. Many of these come to the surface and now seem important. Many retreatants come to realise that God had, indeed, touched their lives down the years in ways they had not been aware of.

Since starting to write this book, I have been reflecting on those years of my life which I have just been describing. My reflection covers a long period indeed, from my boyhood up until about eight years after my ordination. I see it now as a period of struggle between trying to pray on the one hand and following my personal needs on the other. It was, indeed, a wilderness because my prayer never really got going. Yet every now and again there were peak experiences both high and low. Those years were not all black and white, there were flashes of colour too.

Life at a greater depth
Looking back on it now, I see I had other peak experiences that were as overpowering and memorable as when my father died. These peak experiences stand out because, when they happened, there was a heightened awareness of things and a sense of being carried outside myself. They were different from the everyday events of life and had to do with the things of the spirit which we

sense rather than see or touch. It was always in some fleeting way I sensed them and was aware of them. Such events as these can easily pass us by and be forgotten unless we reflect on them or talk about them. For some people these experiences are important and add a new dimension to life. God, or 'The Beyond', seems very close. I wonder if when we experience life at a greater depth like this, does it mean that, in some way or other, we are meeting God? Are these moments contemplative, at least in a broad sense? Are they stirrings of God within us? I'll tell you about some of my own, as they may awaken some of your memories.

The beauty of Connemara

One of my abiding memories is our holidays as students in Clifden in Connemara. I loved those four or five weeks every summer. We used regularly go on cycling excursions. One excursion in particular I remember vividly. It was the day we headed for Renvyle. We cycled to Lettergesh strand. Then we went westwards along a high ridge from where we could see down on a beautiful inlet of the sea. The water was blue and green and there was not a cloud in the sky. There was an atmosphere of warmth around us. We got off our bikes and stood gazing at the scene in wonder. It was ravishing. I felt an ambiance, a presence. We went down to one of those little piers probably built during the famine, and had a swim. Then we ate our meal ravenously. It was idyllic. I wished it would go on for ever. We cycled back to Clifden in brilliant sunshine and when we arrived we were hot and in the mood for a swim. We rushed down to our swimming place and sat down to change. I remember the scene and the atmosphere so well. The sun was beginning to sink into the Atlantic in the west. The sea was calm and the tide was full. I had a sense of fullness and completeness. My joy and contentment were brimming over. Yet this was something more than the sum total of the sky and the sea and the scenery. Again I felt there was a presence of some kind. Was God knocking at the door?

I wonder if my feelings had been heightened by the memory of a passage from Wordsworth's 'Lines written above Tintern Abbey':

The Sounding cataract
Haunted me like a passion; the tall rock,
The mountain, and the deep and gloomy wood,
Their colour and their forms, were then to me
An appetite.

And a little further on Wordsworth, too, senses a presence:

And I have felt
A presence that disturbs me with the joy
Of elevated thoughts: a sense sublime
Of something far more deeply interfused,
Whose dwelling is the light of setting suns,
And the round ocean, and the living air,
And the blue skies, and in the mind of man –
A motion and a spirit that impels
All thinking things, all objects of all thought,
And rolls through all things.

Perhaps many of us do see God in nature. While poetry does not mean as much to me as prose, when I read these lines I think I have some idea of the rapture Wordsworth experienced. I can, too, understand his sense of loss when we are submerged by our mundane pursuits:

The world is too much with us, late and soon
getting and spending, we lay waste our powers.

So just perhaps, in the midst of our laying waste our powers, we can be carried out of ourselves. Again I ask the recurring question, are those the stirrings of God within us?

The house of the dead

Another of these events took place in the city of Galway. One night a few of us cycled down to the university for a lecture. We went down that narrow street past the Franciscan Church. I noticed a big black crepe bow on the door of one of the houses. Someone had died. At one of the upstairs windows the blind was drawn. I could see a light glowing through, obviously a candle. Immediately I began to imagine the scene because it reminded me of my father's death. I imagined every detail of the room. There was, surely, an

old fashioned double bed with snow white bed linen. On the bed
lay the dead man – or was it a woman – dressed in a brown shroud.
The face and the crossed hands were waxen. I could see the bedside
table with a white cloth, a big crucifix and two candles. There was a
smell of death in the room. I pictured men and women and children
sitting on chairs around the walls. It was almost as if I were in the
room. I was transported back to my father's death. And the same
emotions welled up in me. I felt the same sense of loss and loneli-
ness. All that flashed through my mind as we cycled on to the lecture. For the rest of the evening I could not get the scene and the
atmosphere out of my mind. I was once again in the presence of
death. It could have been death anywhere, a universal event. At
that moment I was suffering along with men and women all over
the world who were waking a loved one. Their feelings were mine.

The catharsis

It was at that time, while I was at the university, I met a word that
may describe these emotions within us. Our professor of English,
Professor Murphy, often spoke of the 'catharsis' when we were
studying Shakespeare's tragedies. He was referring, of course, to a
purgation, a surge of emotion, that can be experienced in drama. At
first I did not know what the professor meant. But then when I read
Othello I think I experienced it. Since the play was on the course, I
read it a few times and on each occasion, when I came to the end, I
was carried completely out of myself. I was overcome with shock
and sadness. Poor Othello, poor Desdemona. The tragedy was all so
unnecessary. For me it was summed up in Othello's cry, 'O Iago,
the pity of it.' The play so stunned me and stayed with me for days
that I eventually wondered if this was the catharsis. Plays or books,
apart from 'Love on the Dole', had never had this effect on me
before. I had not courage enough to tell others about this experience. No doubt it was fear of being dismissed. But I did sense that
this was what the professor was speaking of. And it seemed to be
somewhat like the experience of my father's death. And, indeed,
later in life, plays did move me deeply.

In Christ Jesus

I have another abiding memory of a different kind that happened when I was studying theology in Bangalore. It, too, carried me out of myself. For the first time, I woke up to the meaning of a line in scripture.

When reading the letters of St Paul I could not help but notice the phrase, 'In Christ Jesus'. It seemed to appear on nearly every page. I have learned since, in this computer age, that it appears 151 times. So it was obvious the phrase 'In Christ Jesus' was important to St Paul. I asked myself if it could be taken literally? Then I became really excited. Was St Paul telling us the same thing as Christ in the Vine and the Branches? Was he talking about some kind of close union? Now, at that time, we were not conversant with bible dictionaries and commentaries. So I tried to work it out myself. I asked did it mean that we actually are 'in' Christ Jesus; that we literally went into him and became part of him? Could union be any closer than that?

Could it mean further that we actually share the very life of Christ Jesus? St Paul has no doubt but that we share in his death and resurrection. And Marmion used that daring title for his book, *Christ the Life of the Soul*. However, could I go even another step further and say that there is only one spiritual life, that of Christ Jesus? There is only one 'going to the Father' and that is Jesus Christ's. So we, in a sense, have no spiritual life of our own. We actually share the spiritual life of Christ. We are given a *new nature*. St Paul puts it this way: 'And it is no longer I who live, but it is Christ who lives in me'. (Gal 2:20). (See also: 2 Cor 4:10-11).

Was this heresy?

I was very excited by this line of reasoning, but I was afraid it might be heresy. So I typed it out and brought it to my professor of theology. I forget what he said, but he did not reject it. It was only years later, when we were more in touch with biblical scholarship, that I discovered there was a certain truth in what I said.

At the time, it really stirred me. It lifted me out of myself. I worked on it for a long time and it stayed in my mind for ages. I suppose that was the first real beginning of my realisation of our union with Christ. I imagine that theme, union with Christ, became part of the kind of discursive prayer I was trying to follow at that time. And I began to see, also, that union with Christ is what gives meaning to the religious life and what Christianity is all about. Was this another intimation of God in my life?

Had these incidents a deeper meaning?
Looking back on that period from where I now stand, I knew that God was always there. Yet so often he seemed very distant. However, I now realise that he can burst through from time to time. I recall that in all those incidents, there was, indeed, a heightened awareness of things and a sense of being carried out of myself. It was like experiencing life at a greater depth and with great poignancy. The painful events, like the death of my father, were perhaps even more excruciating. But the joyful events, like sunny days or the discovery of scripture, were even more sublime. They were a rapture, a transport. I knew there was something present but it was so big that I could not grasp it. I could only sense it.

The question I am trying to answer is this: when we experience life at a greater depth like that, does it mean we are meeting God in some way? I know, of course, that these glimpses did not always come in what we would call religious or sacred circumstances. But on the other hand God is the ground of our being so the deeper we go into ourselves the closer we come to God. Besides, God is in everything and as a result everything and every circumstance is holy and sacred at its depth. So if we get to the depth of any human experience, there we meet God.

I am sure many people have had similar experiences. Perhaps what I have said will remind them of what they went through and have since forgotten. In later chapters I will look to see if they forecast what I was to experience in the years ahead.

CHAPTER 6

The best of times, the worst of times

I look back on it now as both the best and the worst of times. For one as young and active as I was, externally it was the best of times. I was into my thirties. I loved life in India. I was travelling all over the country on work. I could handle that work well enough and got great satisfaction from it. I was about to return to Ireland for the first time and was looking forward to a marvellous journey to Europe and Ireland.

But there was another side which I could see only in retrospect. I was still in that period which I call 'the prayer of struggle'. That was seven years after my ordination. And it had started in my boyhood. I hope I had matured and grown up in other ways, physically, intellectually, emotionally, sexually, but I seem to have made no real advance in prayer. That is why I think 'prayer of struggle' is an suitable name for this stage. Apart from the few intimations of God I have described in the previous chapter, I never really got going. I knew, of course, that my prayer was not going well. But the real climax had not yet come. So it did not interfere with my relish for life.

Looking back on it now, it was a struggle against my inner tendencies. There were too many other attractions and strong basic needs. I seemed to be constantly failing and making resolutions I never kept. I lurched from one attraction to another right into my mid-thirties. I began to think this struggle would never end.

I imagine that most young people who try to pray go through that struggle in some way or other. It does not make any difference whether they are in a seminary or convent or 'in the world'. And that was not only in the past because I see these same problems in young seminarians and religious today. So in any state of life, this stage must be a hard slog. And usually it goes on for years.

How would I sum it up? There are a few obvious thing I would stress in the prayer of this stage:

It is predominantly vocal prayer

We used the daily prayers we learned by heart, like the Our Father, the rosary and novena prayers. The prayers of the liturgy, the Eucharist and the Divine Office were vocal prayers too. Some carried about their bundles of novena leaflets and memory cards. Of course some form of vocal prayer will, necessarily, continue all our lives. I find I use them everyday.

It is Prayer of Petition

The content of the prayer of struggle is usually petition. We pray for good health, success in an operation, good results in exams, getting a job or a partner in life, and so on.

This emphasis on prayer of petition became very obvious to me when we Irish Redemptorists started the Perpetual Novena to Our Lady of Perpetual Help in 1943 in Belfast. One of the big attractions for the people was the sending in of petitions. Thousands of written petitions used come in every week. They say there are no atheists in the trenches! There were comparatively few thanksgivings. And it is exactly the same at our big novenas today. The petitions arrive even by e-mail. However, we cannot find fault with prayer of petition. After all, Christ advocated it. Ask, knock, seek and you shall receive (Lk 11).

I suppose if someone had suggested we pray in some other way, we would not have known what they were talking about. Prayer of adoration and praise and thanksgiving was scarcely spoken of then.

There may be some form of discursive meditation

Many of us, even lay people, tried hard at meditation and kept at it for years. Some succeeded in the plan I described earlier. They may even have advanced to using scripture, imagining scenes from the New Testament or even entering into the scenes as participants. But even doing that, the prayer still remains discursive. The affective part was so rarely present.

Our human needs win

I think this is the stage where nature will get its way. Without our realising it, nature sees to it that growing up is a more important priority than prayer. Right up until the mid thirties young people are so preoccupied with developing themselves and answering their own inner needs that other things, including prayer, are pushed into the background. Even those who are naturally pious will find prayer a struggle.

What brings this home to me is the fact that I have met many young men, in their late teens or early twenties, who had plenty of training in the prayer of stillness in the novitiate. Indeed, a novice once told me, 'We are long distant runners when it comes to prayer of stillness!' I saw them spend hours in prayer. When they went to the seminary they kept it up for some time. However before long, as far as I could see, they gave up this prayer almost completely. So I realise that, even with the added helps available today, young people are not very different from what we were. Except that we had to continue putting in an appearance at prayer time!

Prayer becomes boring

I am convinced that I became bored at prayer. My prayer remained the same for years. It was like asking an intelligent adult who is a reader to continue reading children's stories or comics. He'd be bored stiff and would not keep it up for long. I was beginning to lose interest.

This is our prayer for life

What made matters worse was a terrible myth. We were given the impression, while students, that this was as far as prayer could go and that we would be praying like this for the rest of our praying lives. To think that that was the whole boring story and it was for keeps!

Dom Cuthbert Butler wrote in 1926, 'It came to be accepted ... that the normal mental prayer for all was systematic discursive meditation according to a fixed method. This was taken to be the lifelong exercise of mental prayer for ... priests, religious, nuns, devout layfolk' (*Western Mysticism*, page 10).

Of course, now and again we did hear that there were a few crack-pots who talked about contemplation and mysticism! We were warned not to dabble in those eccentricities. They could be dangerous. On the other hand, the accepted books at that time seemed to take it for granted that this discursive prayer was the full story and there was nowhere else to go. Indeed, all we could do was get as much as possible out of this discursive prayer. And so there were books like 'Difficulties in mental prayer' that gave us some techniques for handling distractions.

The result is many people have continued praying like this. And no doubt they are pleasing to God. But they say, with false humility, 'Those other forms of prayer are not for a simple soul like me.'And why? Because no one has told them or tried to lead them forward. I think they lose a lot.

The theory

However, there is hope. There is a theory that most of us have to wait until we mature spiritually to be ready for a new development in our prayer. This usually comes some time after the mid-thirties. I read the theory first away back in the 1950s. A man called Demal wrote a book on the psychology of religion, though I have not seen the book in years. He held that conversion usually comes sometime after the mid-thirties. It could, of course, be years later in the the forties or fifties or even later. And he gives very sensible psychological reasons for the theory.

He points out that as we are growing up, we have a lot of conflict within us in trying to come to terms with ourselves. He says it is in our 30s that we begin to get some inkling of who we are, and takes the example of a married man. In his late teens and 20s and 30s his two main drives are his ambition and his sexual urge. He gets a job and marries. In his work, by the time he is in his mid-thirties he has some idea of where his ability lies. He has reached a certain level in his job and has some idea of what his future will be. He knows, too, how far he is likely to go in his social circle and in other spheres of life. So they cease to be a cause of anxiety. As regards his sexual urge, by his mid-thirties he will also have some idea of his sexual prowess and how many children he is likely to have. And that, too, is no longer a major preoccupation. As a result these two cease to be driving forces and so he is relaxed enough to give himself to other things. Often it is to the things of God that he gives his attention.

Indeed, the mid-thirties seems to be the age for maturing in many spheres of life. I was listening to a speaker on the great tenors of this century, from Caruso to Pavorotti. He held that a tenor's voice grew and matured. Most of them reached the heights of their power at about 35 to 40 years of age. So, not only pray-ers but tenors too! Generally it is sometime after the mid-thirties that the big change comes in our lives.

That has been my personal experience as well. As I will explain in a later chapter, the big spiritual change came about in my life when I was in my late-thirties. However, somebody said to me, 'I am past my late-thirties and nothing has happened'! So I stress, for some it could be many years later.

Wasted years?

Does that mean that what happens in the early years is a waste of time? I used often refer to my wasted years of prayer. And yet I do not know. I wonder if I could have really gone deeper into prayer when I was in the trough of the prayer of struggle. Is that what Jesus meant when he said, 'The reason I use parables when talking to them is that they look, but do not see, and they listen, but do not hear or understand'? And Jesus, then, gives the reason from Isaiah, 'because their minds are dull and they have stuffed up their ears and have closed their eyes' (Mt 13:13, 15). Perhaps, because of the struggle, my mind was dull and I did not want to listen.

I wonder then if I could rather describe them as years of necessary preparation. But they were painful years. It was not easy trying to come to terms with myself, as will become clearer later on. My needs were still clamouring to be heard. I was not yet sufficiently at peace with myself to give God my full attention.

Or am I letting myself off too lightly?

Is there any end to it?

So there I was, stuck in this kind of prayer after years and years of struggle. I was not going forward, though I may certainly have been going backwards. I did not know it at the time, but I was coming to a parting of the ways – to a climax.

PART II

The Prayer of Simplicity

The Awakening

When St Teresa of Avila was a young nun she was led into deep prayer, but she began to lead a frivolous life and fell away from praying. In her autobiography she tells us this lasted for about eighteen years. But then gradually the Lord began to bring her back again. It was a turning point, an awakening. And from there she advanced right up to the heights of prayer.

In her last and greatest book on prayer, *The Interior Castle,* she gives a description of a soul going through this awakening. The description is so true to life that I wonder if it is her own awakening she is describing. You will find it in the third chapter of the fourth mansion.

She tells us that the soul, in her journey into the Interior Castle, has wandered away from God. She describes how the soul returns to the castle when she realises how much she has lost. Because she is not worthy to enter the castle, she remains near it. Then the shepherd blows a tune on his pipes. The call is so gentle she scarcely hears it. Yet it is so powerful she learns to recognise this call and does not go away from the castle. She gradually gives up the things that led her astray and eventually enters the castle. Indeed, St Teresa herself is so pleased with this description that she writes, with child-like simplicity, 'I don't think I've ever explained it as clearly as now' (IC 4, 3, 2).

I see this as a good image of the big change that comes into a person's life during the awakening. This awakening comes after the prayer of struggle which I have been describing. It is an intermediate stage of prayer. If one passes successfully though the awakening one enters the fourth mansion.

Notice the sequence in which she describes the awakening.

(1) The soul returns to the castle because she realises how much she has lost.

(2) She hears the call of the shepherd's pipes, which though gentle, she learns to recognise and so does not go away.

(3) Then she gradually gives up the things that led her astray and is ready to enter the castle, that is to go into the fourth mansion where contemplation begins.

This order of events outlined by Teresa rings true to my own experience. I think I went through each of those three stages.

In the 1960s I was changed to the north of India and found myself in charge of a boys' high school. I was seven years ordained but getting nowhere at prayer. I still preferred the cinema to evening meditation. One little incident makes me think there must have been something stirring within me. While I was tied down to the school for most of the year, the other fathers, much to my envy, were travelling around the north of India. Fr John Niall came back from a retreat in Calcutta and told me he was very impressed by a Brother who spoke to him a lot about prayer. I remember saying that I would love to meet him. I must have been dissatisfied with my prayer and felt that if I spoke to someone like him my prayer might improve. There was something awakening within me.

The awakening

Evelyn Underhill, in her comprehensive book entitled *Mysticism*, calls one of her sections 'The Awakening'. And St John of the Cross talks of many awakenings in the spiritual journey (LF 4, 4). Awakening would describe what was happening to me at that time. I had come to the point where my prayer seemed dead and empty. And from what they all said, that was as far as prayer could go. What a fate to be condemned to. Indeed, it seemed my prayer would go on and on in its dreary way for ever and become more tedious in the process. And yet, I was not satisfied. I think I was beginning to feel that there must surely be something more. My present state could not be the full story of prayer or Christianity or God. And what I was seeking was not just little tips on how to overcome distractions at meditation. I wanted a really new insight that would get me going. I was, in effect, to quote Matthew Arnold, 'waiting for the spark from heaven to fall'.

And then the spark from heaven did fall. It happened in Calcutta. The hope of meeting that Brother stayed at the back of my mind. And then one summer I went to Calcutta to give a retreat to the Irish Christian Brothers in their well known school in Bow Bazaar Street. There I met the Brother and the big adventure began for me. He was just an ordinary man with a good sense of humour. What particularly struck me about him was that, when I was with him, he usually spoke of two things: about God and about prayer. Yet he spoke in a way I had never heard before. To him God seemed to be the most wonderful person there is. He spoke of spending hours in prayer, of being so rapt up that the time of prayer passed unnoticed.

Now all that was very different from my struggling experience of prayer. So I listened enthralled. He must have been a marvellous teacher, judging by the way he held my attention. I could have listened to him for ever. Of course, I knew I did not really understand what he was talking about since I had never experienced that kind of prayer myself. But it was stimulating. And so I went off, fired with enthusiasm. I wanted to know God like that. I wanted to pray like that. I wanted to learn more about this kind of prayer he spoke of. The spark from heaven had fallen, indeed.

While I did not get the full import of what this was all about, something had happened. It was as if I were roused from sleep and I awoke to something new and dazzling. I said to myself time and time again, 'deep prayer is possible, because this man and many of his friends are praying that way'. So there was a new hope that my prayer could be different. Those days are frozen into an image in my mind and I can still relive that whole period after meeting him. I was transferred back to Bangalore and I began what was a truly memorable period because it had an atmosphere of its own. It could only be described as a new way of living and praying. Though the Brother's fine words had inspired me, I did not know how to pray in the way he talked of. But I was going to find out and a tremendous enthusiasm carried me along. There were two things I had to learn more about and they were his two favourite topics, God and prayer. A big adventure began.

Who was this God?

I could not get out of my mind the things the Brother said about God. That was probably the first time anyone had spoken to me with real enthusiasm about God. He spoke of him as someone he knew personally. He said, 'Think of the most beautiful person you know; well, God is a thousand times more beautiful.' Indeed, he is Beauty just as he is Intelligence and Power and Majesty. He spoke of the God who keeps us in existence. That I had learned about in metaphysics. God is existence and we share his existence. But the dry metaphysics was now living. It was as if God held us in the palm of his hand and if he removed this support, we would cease to exist. As a result, God is intimately connected with me. He is inextricably bound up with me. He can no more get away from me than I can from him. It is obvious he must love me and care for me.

Often, when I went to pray, I used sit there trying to imagine all this. And of course I couldn't. But I wanted to get closer to this God. Gradually I began to see God as affectionate and loving.

A retreat with a difference

Then another incident took place that helped me see God in the way the Brother spoke of. I made a retreat with a difference. A nun I knew kept telling me about a retreat that had been preached to her community in Belgium. It was by a well known Belgian theologian called Canon Guelluy. I decided to use it for my own eight-day retreat. On the first morning of the retreat I put the typed script on my desk. It was in French. I had a French dictionary on one side and a Bible on the other because it was based on scripture. It turned out to be a marvellous retreat. I still remember so much of it, but it is what he said about God that I remember most. He spoke about how God loved us. I even remember the significant sentence in French: 'Dieu m'aime pour rien', 'God loves me for nothing'. He explained it this way. God does not love me because I am better than others. He does not love me because of the wonderful things I have done, or because of the wonderful things I will do. He loves me for none of these things. He loves me just because I am me. He loves me because he created me. In a word, he loves me for nothing. I thought that was one of the most marvellous things I ever heard about God and me. For a long time when I went to pray, that was my prayer. I kept repeating with wonder, 'God loves me for nothing'. I suppose it was from that there followed for me the beginning of a warmth for God. God gradually seemed closer to me. He became more important in my life. My prayer was beginning to change by being directed to God himself.

Yet, I know now, that this was all heady intellectual stuff. I had not yet experienced the actual love of God for me. However, now at last I had something to pray about.

A new image of Jesus

Another unusual thing for that time was that the retreat was based almost wholly on scripture. Guelluy took up a number of passages from the Bible and drew out of them a message I would never have dreamt of. As a result the verses he spoke of were full of meaning for me. And that whet my appetite. I often used those same passages as my prayer. As a matter of fact I still use some of them. The result was that I began to see Jesus in a new way.

Besides, I think I was still smarting under the taunt of Narindar, a good Hindu friend of mine. He was a teacher in the school in Ambala. He was very religious and used often come to my office after school to talk about religion. When I spoke of Jesus, he dismissed what I had to say. To him Jesus was just another religious leader. He used say, 'Buddhists have their Buddha; Muslims have their Mohammed; Sikhs have their Guru Nanak; and Christians have their Christ.' These were the great religious leaders we heard so much about in India. But I knew there was more than that to Jesus. So I began a big quest to find out how Jesus was different from other religious leaders.

Just at that time I read Durwell's seminal book, *The Resurrection*, and I realised that that is how Jesus is different. Like all the other leaders he died. But then he did something no one else ever did. He arose from the dead.

To understand that more fully, I realised that Jesus was not just God, he was also a full and complete man. He was both God and man. That is the doctrine of the incarnation. If he had not been a man, his passion and death would have been a bit of play acting. So this was his uniqueness. This man died but then he rose again. He overcame death and will never die again. In other words, he was one of us, a human being. And this man Jesus, one of us, is the victor over pain and hunger and thirst and humiliation and death. His rising was not only for himself, it was for us too. We too will arise. Our destiny, as men and women, is changed utterly.

The day I came to realise that was a great day for me. I saw Jesus in a completely different light. I wanted to know more and more about this Jesus, who had changed all mankind. I just knew he must have a deep affection for me. It was the beginning of another aspect of prayer.

Then I knew that Jesus was related to us in another way. Seemingly unrelated ideas from the past began to fit in. You may remember I described how as a student I began to realise that Jesus was the vine, we were the branches. I had to become one with him. The idea of union with Jesus came to the fore again. As I had worked out years before, we are 'In Christ Jesus'. The old became new. My meditations took on a new meaning.

The Psalms

It was just about that time, the early sixties, the vernacular breviary was introduced. I was enthralled by the beauty of the psalms in English; a beauty we missed in the Latin. I remember one morning in the chapel I turned to my companion, Fr Breen, and said to him, 'Isn't that psalm beautiful?' It was one of the usual psalms of praise from morning prayer. The English made a difference because that would never have struck me in the Latin. All this had a great effect on my prayer. Of course, trying to learn more about prayer was part of my experience at that time.

Prayer

When I arrived back in Bangalore, I did not know how to pray in the way the Brother spoke of. But there was one thing I could do and that was read. The Brother spoke of a book that impressed him. It was *The Graces of Interior Prayer* by August Poulain SJ. I found it in our library and used it often. But it lead me to another book that I found even more helpful. It was *The Ways of Mental Prayer* by Lehodey. Lehodey gives an outline of the development of prayer based on St John of the Cross and St Teresa of Avila. As I read it, the early part of his outline was what I had experienced up until that time. I was familiar with the stages of vocal prayer, discursive meditation and affective meditation. But then the big difference came. He did not say that prayer stopped there, as I had been given to understand. Far from it, his outline of prayer continued on and on. Indeed, he was only half way through his book! This is what I had been waiting for, for twenty years. And I could see quite clearly where I had got stuck in prayer down the years. It was right there in meditation, discursive and affective. In my mind a big X marked that spot. So this was to be my starting point. I had to continue from there. You can imagine how avidly I read the rest of the book.

And this, of course, lead me into a completely new world. A world of prayer that went on and on. There was no end to it: one could advance step by step even up to the seventh mansion or the Spiritual Marriage. Of course I felt I would never get that far. But that did not matter. It came home to me that these were, obviously, the stages of prayer the Brother had been talking about. So that made it more accessible. I argued, again, that if he and his friends could reach some of those heights, there might be hope for the likes of me. And I was going to get there!

My prayer began to change

And what a change took place in my actual prayer. Gone was my former boredom. Now I had a goal, something to aim at. And with the world of prayer, the world of God began to open up.

Without anyone telling me, my prayer took on a different pattern. After Canon Guelluy's retreat I often found myself going to the chapel and sitting there just saying from time to time, 'God loves me for nothing'. That simple sentence still filled me with wonder. Or I might find myself reading over a passage from the gospels that Guelluy had explained so well, like the parable of the pharisee and the publican. The refrain, 'God be merciful to me a sinner' would keep sounding in my mind. Or it might be the vine and branches, 'If you remain in me and I remain in you, you shall bear much fruit'. Already there was a yearning to get closer to Jesus. I became more conscious of God's love for me and perhaps one of the psalms of praise would re-echo in my thoughts. 'Praise the Lord, my soul. All my being praise his holy name' (Ps 103). Yet I did not know how to describe that prayer until I discovered that what I was doing was found in Lehodey's next stage of prayer. He called it the Prayer of Simplicity.

Both Lehodey and Poulain emphasise meditation and affective prayer as leading into what they call the Prayer of Simplicity. Each had a chapter on this kind of prayer and I read them time and time again. Indeed, each of them pointed out that this was a significant stage in the development of prayer.

At that time there were no very modern books on this further development of prayer. But I found other precious treasures in the library. They were the other great old classics like *The letters of Dom John Chapman*, Butler's *Western Mysticism*, especially his *Afterthoughts: Bishop Hedley*. Only gradually did I absorb something of what they said. Of course all of these books are based on the writings of St John of the Cross and Teresa of Avila. I only dabbled in John and Teresa in the beginning and it was many years later before I settled down to studying them in detail.

So there I was, about to enter a new stage of prayer. And to think that I had been stuck at the one stage all those years! It was about sixteen years since I was introduced to meditation in the novitiate. I will now have a closer look at the prayer of simplicity.

CHAPTER 8

Prayer of Simplicity

So that was the way forward, the prayer of simplicity. My next task was to find out more about this new way of praying. The name was first used by the French Bishop Bossuet. It is also called the prayer of 'simple regard', from the French word *regarder* meaning to look. Some say this is the type of prayer St John of the Cross is referring to when he speaks of 'a loving awareness' in *The Living Flame,* verse 3, par. 33-35. All the authorities I have mentioned see the prayer of simplicity as the prayer that comes after meditation and before contemplation. So it is often referred to as an intermediate prayer.

What is the change that takes place at this stage? Since the prayer of simplicity should follow meditation, let us see how it is different from it.

What exactly is meditation? As I pointed out before, one begins meditation by taking a text or a passage from scripture and analysing it to get the meaning. Then one applies all this to one's life. This is the discursive part, 'running' from idea to idea. From this should come new ideas and insights leading ideally into affective prayer. Many acts of sorrow or thanks or love can be made to express one's affection for God and Jesus. At its best, meditation was an exercise of tremendous mental activity, with images and thoughts and words and short prayers. Probably the best meditation could be made when one was mentally alert, the imagination flowing.

Our new prayer of simplicity may start off the same way, with a reading. But it begins to be more simple. Instead of frenetic activity there is rather a sense of quiet and peace and calm. There are fewer words or thoughts or images. Indeed, there may be only one predominant idea expressed in a phrase or a sentence repeated from time to time. What is more obvious now is an affection for God. As Lehodey puts it, 'It is an affectionate remembrance of God, a simple loving look at God.' And Lehodey says elsewhere, 'The soul gradually comes to be content with a memory, a look, a glance.' He goes on to say, 'This simple look is always accompanied with love – a love, it may be, almost imperceptible or all on fire.' All that could be summed up in, 'It looks and it loves'. If only we could hold on to these two sentences we would get to the essence of the Prayer of Simplicity.

The soul, then, is content with 'a memory, a look, a glance'. 'It looks and it loves.' There is now a savour for the things of God and the boredom has gone.

And Poulain emphasises how important this stage of prayer is, 'I regard this chapter as being no less useful than the mystic portion, properly so called, of which I am soon to speak' (p. 42).

What Lehodey and Poulain say is full of meaning for me because I lived with those chapters for months and months at that time. That phrase 'a memory, a look, a glance' seemed to sum it up. However, I think that even this beautiful detailed account does not catch the resonance of this prayer. As there are so many forms this prayer can take, I will suggest some of them.

1) The Prayer could be just one sentence

A nun I knew very well told me of an experience which changed her life. She was a prayerful person and at the time was teaching in a girls' school. One day a Sister was giving a lecture to the community. I do not recall what the lecture was about, but during it the lecturer quoted the line: 'Let all that is within me cry holy.' Indeed, she repeated those words a number of times. Unexpectedly the words gripped my friend. They seemed to be full of meaning without her even analysing them. The thought of the majesty and greatness of God overwhelmed her. The words seemed to be saying, God is The Holy, he is The Transcendent, he is The Other. If she were in his presence she would have to cry out 'Holy' since he is so far above us. Not only that, but every part of her being would have to cry 'Holy'. She told me she came out of the lecture in a daze and could think of nothing else but that line. When she went to pray that was her prayer, just repeating, 'Let all that is within me cry Holy.' That line stayed with her for a long time. She told me that she had never experienced anything like that before. Never had she been gripped or held like that. She was convinced that it did not come from herself. The Holy Spirit had something to do with it.

A new awareness
That is the kind of change that comes about in the prayer of simplicity. For years we may have been struggling away at prayer, saying prayers or trying to meditate. Then one day just out of the blue a few lines or a text are unexpectedly full of meaning. There is no need to make a great effort to understand the words. Their meaning is perfectly clear even without analysing them. We see a meaning that goes beyond anything we ever understood before.

But there is another new element – it arouses an affection and a warmth for God. And not only that, it grips and holds us. As a result our prayer may consist only of saying those few lines from time to time.

2) It could be a scene from the gospels
But there is a difference now in the way one would use the gospel scene. In the previous stage of meditation there may have been a lot of activity and movement in the scene, for example in the storm at sea. But now, the scene would more than likely be quiet and calm, more like a still photo. An example that comes to my mind is the famous painting of Jesus in the garden bending over a rock praying, the apostles asleep in the background. There is very little physical movement. Rather, there is a deadly stillness. Let me tell you of a scene I used in my prayer for a long time.

Julian of Norwich
I was stationed in our house in Esker, and one night in bed I was reading The Revelations of Julian of Norwich. This is the account of a series of visions she had over a few days. She saw Christ hanging on the cross in his agony. The vision concentrated on the head of

Christ. It is most graphic writing. She describes how the blood had congealed on the face of Jesus and had become black. Underneath, his face was deadly pale with fresh red blood flowing down. His face was white and black and red. I was reading chapters 21 and 22 of the long version where she tells us Jesus looked as if he were about to expire and she expected him to die at any moment. She looked intently so as not to miss the moment of his death. Just when she thought his life seemed about to end, the expression on his face changed and was now joyful. Our Lord Jesus opened his eyes and said to her, 'It gives me great joy and happiness, it is a perpetual delight to have suffered for you. If I could suffer more I would.' The scene stayed with me for a long time. It became part of my prayer. Often the image of Jesus' face came before me. I used gaze in wonder at his face covered with blood, but yet so joyful. For the first time, I realised it was a delight for Jesus to suffer for me and that he would have suffered more if necessary. Again, a tremendous affection arose within me.

3) It could be a Mantra

The mantra usually appears in this stage of prayer. A mantra is a sound, a word, a phrase or a sentence that is repeated from time to time in prayer. There is no need to analyse it as one would do in discursive meditation. Its meaning is clear to whoever uses it.

The well known Buddhist and Hindu mantra is the sound Om. It signifies God. You often hear a group of Buddhist monks reciting the sound Om, Om, Om. The very resonance of the sound lulls them into stillness. In eastern religions each person usually has his or her personal mantra.

The mantra or the prayer word is also part of the Christian tradition of prayer. The Abbot Cassian advocated it. Then there is the well known passage in *The Cloud of Unknowing*, where the unknown author says, 'If you want to gather all your desires into one simple word that the mind can easily retain, choose a short word rather than a long one. A one syllable word such as God or Love is best. But choose one that is meaningful to you' (Chapter 7). Then the word is repeated during the time of prayer.

There are some well known forms of the mantra. I think the most popular is the 'Jesus Prayer' found in the Greek Orthodox tradition. The short form is the name 'Jesus'. The long form, which is used more often, is 'Jesus Christ, Son of the Living God, have mercy on me a sinner'. Another mantra that has become popular is John Main's 'Maranatha'. This is the last word of the New Testament and it means, 'Come Lord Jesus'.

During the time of prayer one of these mantras is recited from time to time. But there is a progression. It is said first with the lips, then it is said in the mind and finally it re-echoes in the heart. Fr John Main and the advocates of the Jesus prayer suggest that the mantra be repeated during the whole period of prayer.

On a personal note, I find it very distracting to keep repeating the mantra all during the prayer. However, I find it useful to say the mantra for some time when I am distracted. But repeating it all through the prayer makes me numb. Besides when one is led into contemplation the mantra just fades out. However, I know many people find the constant repetition helpful. So I realise it must be a valid and helpful practice.

Of course you can have a do-it-yourself mantra. St Paul seems to suggest one, 'Abba, Father'. Or you could make one from the suggestions in The Cloud, 'God is Love'. The psalms are a good source. I often use, 'Let your light shine on me and I shall be saved.' I like the lines from St John 15, 'If you remain in me and I remain in you, you will bear much fruit.' Another could be the prayer of Bartimaeus, 'Lord that I my see.' Years ago I made up one, taken partly from a charismatic hymn, 'Melt me, mould me, change me.' I often use that other sentence which meant so much to me years ago, 'God loves me for nothing.'

4) The prayer could be just an 'attitude'
At times when we pray we may find that a certain attitude predominates. It could be an attitude of 'awe and wonder' which comes from thinking of the marvel of the universe or of God's love for us. Or we could be bubbling over with 'praise and thanksgiving' because of some wonderful thing God has done for us. Or it could

be an attitude of 'adoration'. Or it could be an attitude of 'sorrow and repentance', when we remember how ungrateful or sinful we have been.

There would be little need to say much. Indeed, not one word need be said. We could just remain in this attitude and that would express the prayer in our hearts. After all, words are not necessary.

5) It could be a deep yearning
But there is one of these attitudes which I must emphasise. It is the attitude of yearning which I feel has an important place as one advances in this stage of the prayer of simplicity. I think there comes, eventually, a longing to be more closely united with God. For me Psalm 41 sums it up: 'Like the deer that yearns for running streams, so my soul is yearning for you, my God.' There is the same longing in Psalm 63: 'O God, you are my God, for you I long; for you my soul is thirsting. My body pines for you like a dry weary land without water.'

As the prayer of simplicity develops, one senses a desire to get closer to God and to enter into deeper prayer. Perhaps this is the climax to the growing affection and tenderness one feels for God. So when at times God seems far away, one can become desperate and the longing deepens into yearning. There is a deep need and want for God. It often strikes me that this is what affective meditation should have lead to. It is only now it comes in the prayer of simplicity. At least for me.

Warning: Beware, distractions still come in this new stage of prayer. What I have described is the prayer of simplicity at its best. But it is not always at its best! At times there can be as many distractions as formerly. Indeed, some speak of being so distracted and agitated that it is impossible to remain at prayer. I generally urge people to struggle on, though at times the best thing may be to leave. However, there are some techniques that may help us get into stillness.

Techniques for getting into stillness
One of the great frustrations of all prayer, and especially of the later

stages, is the difficulty of getting into stillness. We are living in a world of noise and activity. At home there are radios and TVs and computers. Outside there is traffic and aeroplanes and even helicopters. Ours, too, is a world that is achievement orientated. We have lost the way of stillness and silence. And so we carry all this noise within us when we go to pray. As a result we are distracted and even agitated. Yet prayer is supposed to be a refreshment, not a struggle. As Jesus said, 'Come to me all you who labour and are heavy burdened and I will refresh you' (Mt 11:28). Prayer should bring refreshment to body and soul. Yet at times it can be the opposite.

I suggest a few techniques that may be a help. They are, of course, only techniques. They are not in themselves prayer, but they can help us to become quiet and still. You find these techniques mostly in the Eastern tradition of prayer, for example in Transcendental Meditation, Yoga, Zen Buddhism. To a lesser extent they are found in the western tradition such as in Cassian and the *Cloud of Unknowing*. They are so simple we might dismiss them and say, 'Is that all?' Yet they can be a great help.

(a) The position we take at prayer. We should take a fairly comfortable position when we pray because we cannot pray if we are struggling against sore knees or a stiff back. They say the best is the Lotus position, that is squatting as we see orientals doing. However, I think this is a cultural thing. I tortured myself trying to do it in India, but my old bones and muscles were too stiff. Some find a prayer stool very helpful. But, I think a very good position is to use an ordinary straight backed chair. It gives good support to the back. If there is some padding on it, so much the better.

Try to sit with the back straight, the head up, the feet flat on the ground, eyes lightly closed and hands lying on your lap in whatever way you find relaxing. Even the effort of sitting like this at the beginning of prayer is already getting ourselves into the mood for prayer. Soon we will begin to feel the tension draining away.

(b) Breathing. The Eastern traditions lay great stress on the breathing. Deep, diaphragmatic breathing is what we should aim for. Usually our breathing is too shallow. Actually our lungs are quite big and go down to the diaphragm, at the bottom of the ribs. But normally we use only the top part of the lungs. Now, if we keep our shoulders back and expand the ribs, we open up the whole of the lungs and the air rushes in. If we breath like this for some time, we will notice gradually that the slower pace of our breathing has an effect on our mind. For example, if we are frightened or angry our breathing is faster and more shallow. So also when we are calm, our breathing is slower. In deep sleep our breathing is slow and regular. So if we can slow down our breathing and breathe more deeply, our minds become more calm and peaceful.

If we are distracted or agitated at the beginning of prayer, it is a help to spend some time at slow, deep, diaphragmatic breathing. This slows down the body and also has an effect on the mind. You will find that the mind does actually slow down and becomes more peaceful. However, I remember a nun once saying to me, 'I find the breathing a distraction.' So do not let the effort at breathing be a distraction. When the deep breathing has achieved its purpose, when you have calmed down, there is no need to continue.

(c) The Mantra. I spoke of the mantra as a form of prayer. It can also be a help to achieving stillness. It seems to have the effect of distracting the imagination and keeping it quiet. St Teresa talks a lot about the imagination in the way the word is used in scholastic psychology. It is the faculty which pictures things in the mind. It is like a film showing us all kinds of pictures and images. St Teresa calls it the fool of the house. It is not unlike a jester whom kings employed to dance around the house and amuse the courtiers, like our stand-up comics today. We all know that the imagination dances around in our minds distracting us. At times it is better than TV or the cinema! If only we could keep it quiet. I find, if I am very distracted and unable to settle down, repeating a mantra for some time helps me to calm down.

How to pray the Prayer of Simplicity
I suggest: Proceed like in meditation. Sit comfortably. Read a passage from scripture or from a book. Close your eyes and try to get into stillness. Try some of the techniques if necessary, especially the

breathing. Then let things flow. You might find it flows in different ways.

a) If you find the passage or the scene comes into your mind, stay with it.

b) If you find a phrase or a sentence comes, stay with it, repeating it from time to time.

c) If you find yourself becoming still, silent, stay with it. You may find the stillness continues, even getting deeper. You may even get a sensation of sinking deeper. Do not be frightened. Rest in this stillness. This is prayer, deep prayer.

I suggest you continue praying like that every time you go to pray. Just keep at it. You may begin to notice a savour for the things of God that formerly held little interest for you. An affection for God and Jesus may begin to grow in you. Prayer, which before was boring, may become more interesting and even exciting. Why this change in your prayer?

The Holy Spirit has now come to help us

The Holy Spirit has come to help. This is what St Paul is referring to:

'In the same way the Spirit also comes to help us, weak as we are. For we do not know how we ought to pray: the Spirit himself pleads with God for us in groans that words cannot express' (Rom 8:26).

Some think this prayer of simplicity is a mixture of our own effort and the prompting of the Holy Spirit. The awakening is taking place.

How common is the Prayer of Simplicity?

The prayer of simplicity is more common than I ever imagined. I am surprised at how many people come to me to talk about their prayer. They find they are trying to pray more than ever, often after years of not even going to Mass or the sacraments. They want to learn more about prayer and they want to spend more and more time at it. They ask about books or where they can learn. They want to do penance and works of charity. And that is exactly the description that St Teresa of Avila gives of those in her third mansion (IC 3, 1, 5).

It seems to me that her third mansion is really the prayer of simplicity, though the name had not been invented at that time.

When I ask these good people why the sudden interest, they usually tell me they have made a weekend or they have attended a prayer group. Or some traumatic happening took place. They seem to be experiencing some kind of conversion. They remind me of what I went through years ago when I first met the Brother.

Like Lehodey and Poulain, St Teresa sees this as a precious time. She encourages them to desire to advance because God will answer their desire and then she says, 'In my opinion there is no reason why entrance into the final dwelling place should be denied these souls, nor will the Lord deny them if they desire it' (IC 3, 1, 5).

The yearning increases
How long will this stage last? It is different for each person. It could be a short period. A couple of months? A few years? Or St John of the Cross seems to suggest that one could stay there for a long time. Many years. Perhaps one will never pass to the next stage but remain here for the rest of one's life. Of course, as at any stage, one could slip back or give up prayer altogether. This I know only too well from my own experience.

However, at some point in this stage, the yearning I spoke of becomes very strong. One wants to come closer to God. The Lord seems to be preparing one for something more which will lead into a completely different orbit. No doubt this intense prayer of yearning comes as a surprise as it seems to go against the whole trend of the prayer of simplicity. It is no longer simple and still and quiet. Instead it can become a torrent of longing. It becomes a prayer of petition. A flood of words flows. We ask and beseech God for deeper union because we know that there has to be more to prayer than even this prayer of simplicity.

I remember quite clearly going through this period of yearning. I think it is a kind of prelude to the next stage of prayer. We are on the verge of entering contemplation, which I will try to describe in the next section.

PART 3

Contemplation

CHAPTER 9

A New Awareness of God

There I was, after my new awakening, in what seemed to be the prayer of simplicity. But I knew that there had to be something more and I read on about contemplation, which would logically be the next stage. For me this was a period of expectancy that I can recall vividly. A whole new interest had come into my life because I wanted to learn more and more about contemplation. And my yearning for it increased. I often prayed the psalm, 'My soul is yearning for the Lord.' I kept asking 'What is this thing that is called contemplation?' Yet no matter how much I read I could not understand it because I had not experienced it. But I knew it must be something wonderful.

Marmion

I think it was about that time I read the life of the Abbot Marmion by Thibaut. He recounts an incident that happened while Marmion was a seminarian in Clonliffe College in Dublin. Obviously the story had to be told by Marmion himself. One day he was walking along the corridor and unexpectedly he had the experience that God was very close to him. He was so aware of God's presence that he stood still where he was. It must have struck him forcefully, because he never forgot it. In a footnote, Thibaut suggests that this experience of God was the inspiration of much of his writings, especially his wonderful chapter on humility that I read many years ago and still remember. Marmion's point about humility was that we realise our true littleness only when we compare ourselves with the greatness of God. And here Marmion had a little glimpse of the majesty and greatness of God. Fr Mark Tierney, in his recent life of Marmion, relates the same story.

When I read Thibaut's account I knew that something wonderful and unforgettable had happened to Marmion. But what was it? Even Marmion himself did not explain what he went through. However, I realised afterwards that this is what the Brother was talking about. It was contemplation. It was a new kind of praying. It was a new way of seeing God. It was a new awareness of God.

A different way of praying

St John of the Cross starts off by emphasising this. Contemplation is different from the previous stages of prayer. You remember the classic stages of prayer I have described. It began with vocal prayer and praying in our own words. Next followed some kind of meditation. There was discursive prayer which may have led on to affective prayer. Then came the prayer of simplicity, in which 'a thought, a memory, a word' was enough to keep one occupied. (And, by the way, we will constantly be going back to all these forms of prayer even if we are led into deeper prayer.)

Then, apparently at this stage of prayer, something happens deep within us that is not easy to put into words. It is somewhat akin to what Marmion experienced. It is becoming aware of God in a new way. Both John and Teresa tell us it may be a brief experience at first, like Marmion's first experience. It may happen only once or it may be repeated many times during life. But even if it never happens again, one will never forget it. It haunts one for life, as many people have told me. Marmion always remembered that experience in Clonliffe College, though I am sure he had many similar experiences during his life.

I searched to see what other contemplatives have said about this prayer. I discovered that a great source of information is Evelyn Underhill's book, *Mysticism*, in which she quotes from the writings of well known contemplatives down the centuries. Here are some of the accounts that struck me. I use her translations though they are quaint and clumsy.

She quotes St Bernard who said, 'The Word has visited me and even very often. But though he has frequently entered my soul, I have never at any time been sensible of the precise moment of his coming. I have felt that he was present, I remember that he was with me. I have sometimes even been able to have a presentiment that he would come: but never to feel his coming nor his departure' (Underhill, p. 244).

Hugh of St Victor describes the Soul speaking: 'Tell me what can be this thing of delight that merely by its memory touches and moves me with such sweetness and violence that I am drawn out of myself and carried away ... I am suddenly renewed: I am changed: I am plunged into ineffable peace. All my pain is forgotten ... I seem to have become possessed of something, I know not what it is' (Underhill, p. 245).

Then Evelyn goes on to use her own words to describe contemplation. She asks what this illumination is that they talk of? She answers, 'They do experience a kind of radiance, a flooding of the personality with new light. A new sun rises above the horizon and transfigures their twilight world. Over and over again they return to this light imagery' (Underhill, p. 249).

And yet, she tells us, this does not take away from their everyday duties. 'The mind concentrated on a higher object, is undistracted by its own anxieties, likes or dislikes; and hence performs the more efficiently the work that is given it to do ... St Teresa was an administrator of genius and an admirable housewife and declares that she found her God very easily among the pots and the pans' (Underhill, p. 246).

A summing up

Perhaps from these passages I began to form some kind of a picture of what contemplatives experience. They sense that in some way God is present with them although usually nothing is seen or heard. They do not know how the presence comes or goes. When the experience is over they apparently have nothing to show for it, yet they are absolutely certain that it took place. Often there remains an elation and a glow, a joy and a peace. It is as if a fragrance or an aura lingers on. Even the memory of it moves them. They know they are changed. Even if this never happened again, they will never forget it. It is indelibly printed on their memory.

Contemplation in scripture

There was still another source to search. True, the word contemplation is never mentioned in scripture, yet there are a few passages in the New Testament that make me wonder if deeper prayer is indicated. It is, of course, the prayer of Jesus that dominates the gospels and his prayer is based on his relationship with his Father. And Luke tells us, 'But he would go away to lonely places where he prayed' (Lk 5:16).

I have often wondered how Jesus actually prayed on these occasions. There are some passages that may give us an indication. The transfiguration struck me.

1) The Transfiguration

I will take Luke's version in chapter 9:28-36, since he places the scene in a prayer setting. 'Jesus took Peter, James and John with him and went up a hill to pray' (v. 28). Perhaps this was going to be one of his usual night sessions of prayer. And indeed it did turn out to be a glimpse of Jesus at prayer. Luke tells us, 'While he was praying, his face changed its appearance and his clothes became dazzling white' (v. 29). Then Moses and Elijah were with him discussing how he would die in Jerusalem, his 'exodus'. Peter and James and John had been asleep but awoke and saw Jesus' glory and the two men with him. Now was this an example of the way Jesus usually communed with his Father? Was it one of his usual mystical experiences? McKenzie says this must be taken as ecstatic in character. It seems, too, to have been contemplative for the three apostles. Then a cloud, which is a sign of God's presence, covered them and a voice said from the cloud, 'This is my son whom I have chosen – listen to him.'

Was that typical of the way Jesus prayed when he was alone?

2) Paul's Vision (2 Cor 12:1-10)

The background to this passage is interesting. St Paul seems reluctant to speak of his vision. He does so only to answer those who said he was not a true apostle. Those opponents are mentioned in the previous chapter (11:5). They boasted of their credentials to be apostles and this included visions and revelations. They seemed to imply that Paul had not these credentials and at that Paul bristled. So he went on to prove that he too could boast of visions and revelations. Yet he did not say clearly that he was the man who had the visions. However, most commentators take these experiences as being his own because of the precision with which he timed them, fourteen years earlier. He tells us that this man, Paul himself, was snatched up to the highest heaven, though whether bodily or not he did not know. And there he heard things that cannot be put into words. It seems to me that this was some kind of a contemplative experience. It sounds like a rapture.

This may give us some flavour of one aspect of contemplation, the joyful experience of God.

The other side of contemplation

But I had to keep reminding myself that this is only one side of the story, the delightful part of contemplation. St John of the Cross keeps emphasising that there is another side. It is the suffering of purification. So this prayer is both the agony and the ecstacy. Jesus experienced the same thing. The glory of his resurrection came only after his suffering and death. And it will be the same with us as Jesus made clear to his disciples. You remember the story which is found in Matthew 20.

The mother of James and John came to Jesus and asked if her sons could have a place, one at his left and one at his right, when he was king. Jesus said, 'You do not know what you are asking for.' Then Jesus asked the sons directly, 'Can you drink the cup of suffering that I am about to drink?' 'We can,' they answered. 'You will indeed drink from my cup,' Jesus told them, 'but I do not have the right to choose who will sit at my right and at my left' (Mt 20:21-23).

It took me, too, a long time to realise that when we are invited into contemplation, Jesus is asking us the same question, 'Can you drink the cup of suffering that I am about to drink?' Like James and John, we want the glory and joy and sitting in the place of honour. As for the chalice, we too think we will take that in our stride. Little do we realise that it may be more than we can bear. True, the

Brother had been talking about the suffering and the purification
we have to go through. And Lehodey, following John of the Cross,
leaves us in no doubt. However, at the beginning I did not get the
full import. At first I felt it would be good to get to know my weaknesses and faults even if it meant suffering. Of course, I thought
Jesus was referring to some grand, noble sufferings which I would
certainly know came from God. I imagined there would be something heroic about them, and so I could take pride in my martyrdom! Little did I know the bitterness that is part of this way of
prayer.

A parish priest and the Little Flower

It brings to my mind the story of the parish priest who read about
the *Little Way* of the Little Flower. He had tried other ways of spirituality but they did not work for him. But when he read the Little
Flower he told his friends, 'This is the way for me.' So he got down
to practice: like the Little Flower he was going to be the little toy the
Father would cast aside from time to time. It was all going very well
at first. After a couple of months someone asked him, 'How are you
getting on with the Little Flower?' He said, 'When you get down to
it, she's as hard as the rest of them!'

Fears about contemplation

Yet I approached this new way of praying with nervous excitement
and apprehension. However, what I knew about contemplation
was sketchy. I was aware, of course, that it was looked upon with
suspicion but that made it alluring yet menacing. As a schoolboy, I
heard an old priest saying that he met a lady who talked of contemplation. He told us it was a dangerous thing to dabble in! There was
a fear that hidden demons could be unleashed within us.

And Dom Cuthbert Butler, in his classic book *Western Mysticism*,
confirms that that attitude was common early this century. 'This
contemplation ... had come to be regarded as wonderful, even
miraculous; to be admired from a safe distance, and left alone as
dangerous and full of pitfalls' (p. 10). And that attitude of distrust
still persisted when I first became interested in it. The general idea

was that if Christians practiced vocal prayer and meditation they were doing all right! Indeed, contemplation was never discussed in ordinary church circles at that time, though there had been a big debate going on, early in the century, in learned theological circles, between Poulain and Sandreau and Garrigou Lagrange and others.

So after I became aware of contemplation, I scarcely used the word when giving retreats to priest and religious. I think the reason for this mistrust was that it was often confused with what were called the 'extraordinary phenomena' of mystical prayer. These were experiences that some saints and holy people had, like visions, levitation, bilocation, the stigmata, ecstasies in which one became rigid or impervious to burning and pain. These things are indeed extraordinary and are not part of the ordinary way of prayer. There is a well-known book on these extraordinary phenomena by a Mgr Farges. True, St John of the Cross speaks of some of them. However, he advises us to pay no attention to them, even if they do seem to come from God! The reason he gives is that these things are not a proximate means of union with God. And union with God is what counts. I personally give no encouragement to people who tell me of visions and such things. So I would like to assure the reader that there is nothing unusual about contemplation. Indeed, for many it is simply the next stage of prayer that God leads them into. Though there is a controversy about whether all or only some people can be led into contemplation, I will not go into that here.

What proof?
There is another difficulty. Some people ask what proof there is that these experiences really take place. Now, we cannot prove them in the way we can prove that something physical exists, or that two plus two makes four. But there is the witness of contemplatives all down the centuries and indeed in all religions. A constant and compelling witness it is too. I suppose it is like the resurrection. We may have our doubts, and few of us escape those, yet we accept it or we don't.

Contemplation is a way of life

On the other hand, contemplation is unlike any of the previous stages of prayer in still another way. It is in a different league altogether. I think contemplation should have a warning like the health warning on cigarette packets: 'Beware, contemplation is dangerous'. It is dangerous because it is not just a way of prayer, it is also a way of life. It can begin to take over more and more of our life just like cards or golf or drink or computers or other addictions! Contemplation can change our outlook and as a result our lifestyle. That scares some people and often frightens them off. I have often heard people saying, 'I am afraid of what the Lord is going to ask next!'

Contemplation, then, is not like the previous stages of prayer. We enter a completely different way of praying. It is a quantum leap, a sea change. A new consciousness of God is beginning. It becomes a search for union with God. As a result, love of God becomes important. As St Teresa says, 'the important thing is not to think much but to love much'.

So there I was on the verge of something wonderful and yet something painful. But this was all theory. I was yearning for something to happen, but I was apprehensive. And then it came.

CHAPTER 10

A Biographical Interlude

A lay person who read the manuscript of this book remarked that I was constantly quoting St Teresa of Avila and St John of the Cross. She told me she knew nothing about them and suggested it would be helpful if I added a few details about their lives.

St Teresa of Avila (1515-1582)
St Teresa was a Spaniard, born into a well-off family in Avila in 1515. She grew up hearing about the doings of Henry VIII and Martin Luther and later Elizabeth I. She entered a Carmelite Convent and soon got into deep prayer, but gradually she began to lead a giddy life and gadded around the convent gossiping. She fell away from praying. She tells us this lasted for about eighteen years and then, with the help of others, she came back to prayer. This time she threw herself into prayer so earnestly that she became one of the great contemplatives.

With that came the desire for a stricter life. She founded the strict Reformed Carmelitie Sisters we are familiar with today. She had a magnetic personality and attracted so many to join her that she travelled about opening convents. She was known everywhere, not unlike Mother Teresa in our day. One of her great conquests was John of the Cross, a Carmelite priest. He agreed to join her reform.

She wrote many books, though where she got the time I do not know! She told the story of the founding of her houses. She wrote her autobiography in which she related how her prayer developed. Her last and greatest book was *The Interior Castle*, also called the Book of the Mansions. In it she described the development of prayer right from the earliest stages up to 'mystical marriage'. The image she takes is that of the soul advancing from room to room in the castle. There are seven mansions in all. It is in the fourth mansion that one enters contemplation. Then the prayer goes deeper in the fifth mansion. In the sixth and seventh mansions she describes the love story of union with God in the 'spiritual betrothal' leading to the 'spiritual marriage'. This is the highest stage of union with God. All through this journey she relates her own personal experiences of prayer.

All her books, and especially *The Interior Castle*, are looked on as spiritual classics. In her autobiography, chapters 11 to 21, there is the well known *Four Waters*. This is a description of her four stages of prayer using the analogy of four ways of watering a garden. But after writing that she advanced even more in prayer. *The Interior Castle* was her last book and her final word on prayer.

Though she is very long winded and goes off on tangents, she is fresh and readable. Indeed, she is much more readable than John of the Cross, because she tells her own experiences. I thought at first I would find her hard going, but I soon got used to her style. I encourage you to read her.

St John of the Cross (1542-1591)

John's early history is very different from that of Teresa. He, too, was a Spaniard. His father married his mother against the approval of his family. Then he died young and left his wife with three small children and she got no help from her husband's family. So John was brought up in poverty. But he was very bright and became a Carmelite. He was a very good theologian. However, he was seeking a life of deeper solitude and prayer and had been thinking of joining the Carthusians when he met Teresa. She told him she was about to reform the Sisters to the primitive stricter rule. He said he would join her. He and a companion opened a house of the discalced Carmelites in Duruelo in 1568 against much opposition.

Then he had a terrifying experience. On 2 December 1577 he was captured by his fellow Carmelites who demanded he renounce the reform. John, of course, refused. So he was declared a rebel and imprisoned in a monastery in Toledo. He was kept in a little cell and practically starved. He was taken out from time to time to be scourged before the whole community. But when he was brought out he studied the lie of the land and made his preparations. Then one dark night he escaped and turned up like a scarecrow at one of the convents of the nuns who looked after him. The reform flourished.

It was while he was in jail that his spiritual doctrine developed. He is, of course, one of the great poets of Spain. His spirituality was expressed first in poetry. His most famous poem is based on his jail experience and on his escape. It is called 'On a Dark Night'. He describes how the soul is led into contemplative prayer on a dark night, in the obscurity of dark faith. But what puts many people off is his demand that the soul must tend to seek the 'Nada', nothing.

He read and explained the poems to the nuns and friends for whom he wrote them. Then he wrote commentaries. The longest of his poems is 'The Spiritual Canticle'. It has forty verses with a commentary on each verse. In this poem he traces the development of the relationship of the soul with God, through the purgative, the illuminative and unitive way. He ends with a beautiful description of the spiritual marriage.

At first I found St John hard going and as dry as dust. But I persevered, encouraged especially by some sections that tallied with my own experience. While I like Teresa's writings, I find I get more out of St John. I go back to him time and time again. Indeed, I find the actual text more helpful than many of the learned commentaries I have read!

John's health began to get worse and he had open sores from the earlier scourging. At the end he bore with patience the harsh treatment of an unsympathetic superior. He died in Ubeda in 1591.

CHAPTER 11

And then the Lord came

I can still remember those days in Bangalore. I continued trying to find out more about contemplation and I was yearning for it to come. I kept reading what Lehodey and John of the Cross had to say about it. Besides, my life was full. Vatican II was in full swing and I read all that the papers, religious and secular, had to report about it. Those who lived through those years would understand how all-engrossing every bit of news and gossip from Rome was.

I went out on missions. I gave retreats to nuns and brothers and priests. When I was on those missions and retreats I spent a lot of time in personal prayer. Canon Guelluy's retreat gave me a new image of God and got me interested in scripture. And, of course, I continued doing a lot of study on scripture because Fr Sean Kelleher's seminars on scripture made the Bible more living. The breviary in English, too, made the psalms more prayerful. And the more I studied prayer, especially contemplation, the more I yearned for it to come.

An experience of God
And then it came when I was not expecting it and in a way I had never anticipated. And although it came many times later in my life, that first occasion remains special. I have already told this incident in my first book, *The God of Welcomes* (p. 134), so I will not repeat all the details again.

Of all places it happened on a crowded train. I was giving a retreat to sisters in the town of Quilon, which is on the south west coast of India in the state of Kerala. The morning the retreat ended I had to go to Madras, though I did not know what for. The nuns got me down to the station before the train arrived at 6.30. It was packed though eventually I got into a second class carriage but could not find a seat. However, up high there was a berth free so I spread my bedding and lay down on it. This was the usual procedure in India as the journeys could be very long. I did not mind the long journeys because I am a great reader and lay there reading probably one of the latest novels. And then it happened.

Unexpectedly I had a sense of God being present. A tremendous stillness and silence descended on me. Everything seemed to stop. It was as if I were taken out of myself. I was utterly and completely absorbed in this sense of presence. Of course I saw nothing or heard nothing but I knew that God was present in some way. And he seemed to be the most wonderful person I had ever encountered. I knew with absolute certainty that he loved me and cared for me. And not only that, I felt certain that everything said in the New Testament was addressed directly to me. I knew I was accepted by God. I had never experienced a peace and calm like this before. I was content to remain that way, absorbed in whatever it was.

I lay there and put my book aside as my interest in it had gone. I was happy to give myself up to whatever this presence was. The hours passed and I longed for it to go on and on and it did. At one point I took up the New Testament and tried to read it, but I was too overwhelmed to concentrate on any particular part of it. When we stopped at stations I went on to the platform and had a cup of coffee. Some time during the evening when we came to a meal station, I got some curry and rice. And still the presence went on. When night came I fell asleep though I did, as usual, wake up at noisy stations. And even then my first thought was of this God who was present with me.

We arrived at Madras central station about 5.30 the next morning and when I awoke the sense of presence was still there. As I did not know what work I was supposed to do in Madras, I went in search of a Redemptorist and found one giving a retreat to the Presentation Sisters in Vepery. I was still so conscious of the presence of God that I was sure it would be obvious to him. But, of course, it wasn't. I did find out where my superior was and what work he wanted me to do. The sense of presence continued even after I returned to our monastery in Bangalore.

Yet all the while I wondered if this was a valid experience. So eventually, after many attempts, I went to one of the fathers who taught me theology when I was a student and told him about it. I was wondering if he would tell me to go off and have a bit of sense. But he took me seriously and so I felt reassured and encouraged.

A new phase in my life

Thus began a completely new phase of my life, a delightful period. I have a few entries in my diary about that time but unfortunately they are badly written and hard to read. While I have not total recall, these entries bring back to my memory something of the atmosphere I lived in at that time. Naturally my interest in prayer increased and, indeed, it became the centre of my life.

When I was at home in the monastery, I tried to spend as much time as possible at prayer, either in the oratory or in my room. I used look forward to those sessions of prayer and what a change that was. I suppose in the beginning I hoped to recreate what had happened on the train. But I soon discovered that stillness and absorption cannot be summoned up at will. They come in God's good time. I think I did learn quickly enough that the best I could do was to remain as quiet as possible. But that was easier said than done. Very often I could not settle down to prayer. My head was full of distractions and that was frustrating. At other times it was sheer delight. I see a note in my diary, 'What a surprise that God has not left me!'

True I had been trying to pray before this experience on the train took place, but there was a mighty difference now. I would usually begin my prayer with a reading from scripture and then allow myself to get into stillness. But the prayer proceeded in many different ways. Sometimes I found it difficult to remain still. Sometimes I was distracted and agitated just like of yore.

But at other times the stillness would come upon me quickly enough. I remember describing it this way. I would have a feeling of sinking and going deeper in consciousness. Then what I had experienced on the train came back. There was that same sense of being absorbed and held and I could be gripped like that for some time, even for a long time. On other occasions I had feelings of ardent love for God and gratitude for what he was doing for me.

All this still surprised me. I was going about in a daze, in a different world. And the Lord still stayed with me.

I kept reading Lehodey, Poulain and the others to see how they described this further stage of prayer. Of course, I was trying to judge how far I had really advanced and that is a temptation for all of us! I asked myself, was my prayer like what they said? What stage had I reached? I studied St John's map of the ascent of Mount Carmel. But there were so many things they said that meant nothing to me. And then I wondered if I was advancing at all and felt discouraged.

Doubts

I see too, from my diary, that I had plenty of doubts. The first and most persistent one was, 'Why me'? I often felt I did not deserve this gift and that the Lord would go away. I suppose everybody who is led into contemplation feels that and needs a lot of reassurance. But then, I see from my diary, I would thank God for the joy of being loved and being loved for nothing. However, when I thought of the gift God gave me, I was conscious that I was unfaithful. For example, I was thinking too much about myself and little about others. For parts of the day, I did not even think of God, and I felt that was a true sign that I did not love him enough. I was smoking far too much and despite all my efforts I could not, or would not, give it up. And, of course, my old fault, I still longed to be praised especially for my sermons and I was often jealous of others who seemed to do better. I gossiped and did not even try to help others. I seemed to become more and more selfish. My faults, far from diminishing, were multiplying. And yet I reasoned with myself that God did not want us to be without faults but rather to recognise that we have them and still accept that he loved us without limit. Simple though that may seem, doubts of his love for me still came.

I remember saying often to my director, 'If God took away this gift, I do not know what I would do.' He used say to me, 'You would just keep on going as you are.'

And of course my work went on in parallel with this. I was constantly out on missions and retreats. That meant writing new sermons and conferences and I had plenty of new material after my recent experience and study and the documents of Vatican II. Naturally I preached on prayer very often and yet never mentioned the word contemplation! It just was not done.

My work load increased

I was really leading the life of a contemplative. I remember what my ideal was, to be a contemplative in the market place. If only I could lead both the active missionary life and the contemplative life. That, indeed, did go on for a number of years. I look back on those years as the glory days. Shortly after these events, my life changed in another way. I was appointed Rector of our house in Bombay and I became involved in administration. I kept up the prayer for a number of years, but the work load increased. And so gradually I paid less and less attention to prayer and bit by bit fell away from it. Then after six years as Rector in Bombay, I was elected Vice-Provincial of our Vice-Province of India and as we were practically autonomous that really meant being Provincial. I was on the move much of the time visiting all our houses in India and Ceylon, as it was then called. My prayer was getting an even bigger battering. After three years as Vice-Provincial, I returned to Ireland and was almost immediately appointed Rector of Marianella, our house in Dublin. What a change from India to Ireland. And that was a big job too, with a community of up to fifty. Besides I was in charge of our mission team for which I had to organise all the work. I was so preoccupied with these jobs that I continued to pray very little.

However, my conscience was not at peace. I still yearned for deeper prayer. And then the catalyst came. The occasion was a retreat many of us Redemptorists made together in Limerick. Once again I heard the pipes of the shepherd. I returned to Marianella and made a little prayer room at the top of the house. I got into the way of going to pray there frequently and that lengthened into hours. I am still amazed at this gift of God after being unfaithful for so many years – I think it was about ten years in all. But now I was

back to prayer and into reading John of the Cross and Teresa of
Avila. And the prayer has continued since with the usual careless-
ness and low points and high points.

What I have been talking about here is the joyful side of contemplation. But, as I pointed out, there is another side – the purifications
which I will deal with in the next chapter.

CHAPTER 12

The purification of our human weakness

Canon Guelluy tells a story that is appropriate here. After World War II there was a young married couple living in Belgium. They soon discovered they could not have children and they wanted a family. So they decided to adopt a child. At that time, after the war, it was easy enough to get children for adoption. So they went to different orphanages and saw so many beautiful children that they could not make up their minds. They were looking for the perfect specimen. In one orphanage a nun was showing them around. She passed a room in which they noticed a cot and they asked to see the child. The nun said she did not bring them in because any one who saw the child did not want to take it. The young couple soon realised why. The child was handicapped. After much discussion they decided to take it in preference to all the others. When the nun asked why, they said they were heart broken at the thought that no one ever wanted to take the child. They knew they were probably the only couple who would give the child the opportunity of being brought up in a normal family.

I am the handicapped child
I gradually began to realise that I, too, was the handicapped child. And I still am. I am only too aware of my weaknesses and faults and compulsions. Like St Paul, I found myself doing the very things I did not want to do. Despite my efforts, all my resentments and jealousies and compulsions and self indulgence remained.

But now I realised another aspect of my handicap: God was waiting for me, even though I was handicapped. Of course we are all handicapped and yet God actually wants each of us, handicap and all.

It was John of the Cross who made me aware that I was indeed handicapped. Of course, at that time, I would have admitted that I had a few faults just like everybody else! But on the whole I was not too bad! With a little bit of self control and discipline, I'd straighten them out. Perhaps it would not be all that difficult.

Besides, I wanted to get down to the real thing. I wanted to read about God and prayer and above all I wanted to experience deep prayer. I'd see about those few faults later. But here John stepped in and helped me realise that there were many things to attend to first and how! My whole way of life was about to be turned upside down by the process.

An accurate description
St John, in his *Dark Night*, Book 1, gives us a precise and marvellous description of the person who has reached this stage of prayer and is on the verge of advancing along the road. I can see myself, and many people I met later, in this sketch. I will paraphrase what he says.

The soul, he tells us, has gone through new experiences that have changed him. He has discovered God and prayer. He now finds his joy in spending hours at prayer, perhaps even entire nights. He is happy doing penances and fasts. He goes to the sacraments often and loves talking about spiritual things (DN 1, 1, 3).

That is so true even today. In this age of organisations and groups, I meet many people who have had such a conversion experience. They spend hours at prayer meetings and healing Masses. They think nothing of travelling for miles on pilgrimages, and even praying for an entire night. The hardship involved does not upset them. They search out spiritual functions to attend. Indeed, I have had to restrain their penances and fasts. And yet, in a way, I have to admire them. Then St John explains why they have advanced so far.

He tells us that these beginners, as he calls them, have tried to live good lives and have persevered in meditation and prayer. It is through this attachment to prayer that they get satisfaction and become detached from worldly things. They get strength to control their appetites and put up with suffering. They are doing very well.

But then all changes!

It is at this time, 'when in their opinion the sun of God is shining most brightly on them', that things begin to happen (DN 1, 8, 3). True they are very good people, but they think they are more advanced than they are. But John points out they have a lot more to learn about prayer and even more about themselves.

He goes on to say they often practice these things for the consolation and satisfaction they get out of them. Yet they have many faults and like children they have not acquired firm habits of virtue (DN 1, 1, 3). Then John proceeds to list their human weaknesses. Here, I think, he hits the nail on the head! I find it quite devastating because it is a good description of what I am myself. I think John has some marvellous insights. Here are some of them:

Our human faults

   * These beginners become vain and want to appear holy. They love instructing others. Gradually they think they do this better than anyone else.

   * They become very jealous and dislike praising others. They become ambitious and want to be at the head of their group.

   * They feel they are very humble until their pride is hurt! Then they refuse to give in.

   * They become self righteous and get angry at the sins of others. They want to lead crusades to combat the sins of today. They will fight great battles against drink and drugs and glue-sniffing and pornography and divorce and abortion. Being out with a placard in their hands would make them happy!

   * They get angry with themselves. However, they regret their faults mostly because they have let themselves down. You know, they say the most difficult person to forgive is myself.

   * They suffer from spiritual gluttony. They want to spend more time at prayer meetings. They cannot get enough night vigils and pilgrimages. They even neglect their families and essential work (DN 1, ch 1-7).

Some concrete examples

Like all of us, they do not realise they have these faults. Let me give you some examples that I have met:

* *Power tastes sweet!* In a certain group, the year of office for the leaders was over and new ones were elected. However, the old leaders refused to relinquish office. A bitter battle followed. In desperation the bishop sent a priest to settle the quarrel. The old leaders still refused to accept their legitimate successors. Power tastes sweet and it is hard to give it up. Eventually the bishop suppressed the group. And, you know, they were all prayerful people.

* *Our group is authentic!* I know an organisation that was thriving, attracting many. Then different interpretations of the movement were put forward. The members divided into two groups, and each group held they had the authentic interpretation. A power struggle followed. Though all had been friendly before, they became quite vicious with each other. In a very short time the organisation collapsed. It no longer functions. And they had been doing great work.

* *We are not talking to you!* In another group, a few very enthusiastic members had a misunderstanding with some of the others. It lead to a bitter argument. They walked out of a meeting and refused to come back in spite of many appeals. Their pride had been hurt, though I doubt if they would have been ready to admit that.

* *Let me be a martyr!* A Salesian in India told me the story of a confrere who was a bishop in China. He eventually had to give up his diocese and arrived in India. Obviously he had a great sense of humour. One of the Salesians asked him if he found it hard to leave his diocese. He answered, 'It is very hard to get up on the cross, but it is even harder to get down from it!'

John of the Cross wants us to notice all these things that are going on within us: the vanity, the jealousy, the pride, the spiritual gluttony, the clinging on to power. And yet we find it hard to admit these faults, even those that may be obvious to others. We feel we are not as bad as all that.

Self knowledge

And so God takes a hand in helping us to know ourselves and admit our faults. He does this because these weaknesses and selfish longings so preoccupy us that we cannot hear him. His only hope, then, is to shock us into coming face to face with our true selves. Especially at the beginning of contemplation, he will allow painful situations to arise that will force us to know ourselves. These situations will be so hurtful and so crowd in on top of us that we cannot miss them. And perhaps the heightened sensitivity of that time makes them more bitter.

It was only when the purifications came that I realised the process of self knowledge is an integral part of the whole spiritual life. They were God's way of forcing me to admit that I was the handicapped child.

St Teresa on self knowledge

St Teresa is very keen on our knowing ourselves. She writes, 'This path of self knowledge must never be abandoned ... There is no stage of prayer so sublime that it is not necessary to return to it' (Life, 13, 15).

John of the Cross emphasises the same point. He keeps pointing out that we must recognise our faults, otherwise they will prevent us from advancing in prayer. Hopefully these sufferings will make us realise how much has still to be purified in us.

Noble sufferings

I remember when the Brother told me of these purifications I thought they would be noble sufferings, evidently bearing the mark of God. And that would make them bearable. And others would at last come to understand what I had been going through all along!

However, when the sufferings came they were not at all like that. They were small and petty and often sordid and vicious and always humiliating. There was no evident trace of God in them. Indeed, quite the opposite. It was often a matter of others being vindictive and out to get their own back. Indeed, as we go through the sufferings, we can almost hear others gloating in the background.

An incident like that happened to me when I was just about about entering this period of prayer.

I am not into journal keeping but I have a couple of diaries in which I take notes during retreats or at high points in my life. Recently, I read an entry I had completely forgotten. But now that it has come back to my memory, it sends a shiver down my spine. At the time it seemed very vicious and hurt me deeply.

The Karachi Mission

We Redemptorists in Bangalore were asked to preach a series of missions in Karachi which was at that time the capital of the two wings of Pakistan. A number of us were appointed to go. I was very pleased when I was asked because I had never been there and the opportunity did not turn up often. When I arrived in Karachi, my first mission was in a small parish on the outskirts of the city. Then all of us joined together in the cathedral in the centre of the city where we had to do a lot of visiting. It was the first time I had worked among so many Muslims and I found it a completely different culture. As usual I enjoyed being in a new place.

Since a number of us were there together in the one church, we had not so much preaching to do. I remember I did not get preaching on the subjects I would have liked. But that was the way it worked.

When the mission was over I eventually returned to Bangalore, pleased at how all the missions had gone.

I was not back very long when the Rector sent for me. He was sitting at his desk with a letter in his hand. He told me he had received a letter from one of the priests in Karachi. He said to me, 'And you think you are a great missioner! Well in this letter the priest says he does not think much of your efforts nor of your preaching.' He implied that the other missioners were far better than I was and that I was a failure.

I could not believe it. This was my job and something I worked hard at. And now I was told I was useless at it. I was confounded. The bottom seemed to fall out of my world. But what made it worse was the way the message was delivered. I knew the Rector very well as we had lived together in a small house for a few years. He was a good friend of mine and a kind man. Now, I may be wrong, but he sounded spiteful. It was as if he meant to hurt me and leave me in no doubt as to his message.

I have a few other little notes in my diary that are badly written and hard to decipher. But this I can make out, 'When the Rector mentioned it, I was thrown into a dark despondency.' I am always sensitive to being dismissed like this.

But then, as so often happens in religious communities, news got around. I knew that others were talking about it. I need hardly tell you I did not spread it as I was too ashamed to let others know of the letter. However, there was one man I could speak to and I told him about it. But I can judge how hurt I was by still another note in the diary. A very good friend of mine asked me about the incident. I told him I was so upset that I would prefer to leave it alone for the time being. And that is not like me. I prefer to talk things out.

Obviously it had gone very deep and was still rankling within me. I was humiliated. I see from the diary that I tried to tell myself that this was the will of God for me. But that did not calm me. I was boiling with anger and squirming with shame. I could not accept it as coming from God because all I saw was the spitefulness of others. I am sure I struggled with that for a long time, because that is the way I am. It takes me a long time to get over hurts and humiliations. Indeed, the thought of that incident still makes me squirm.

Incidents like that taught me the lesson John wanted me to learn. Gradually I began to realise how much of self and pride and jealousy and touchiness there was still in me.

Was that a pattern?

And that seemed to be a pattern at that period. Incidents like that came from time to time and that right down the years. Just when I seemed to be getting on all right and my work going fairly well, they happened. A little remark from someone and the whole train of reactions started again. It was always a great struggle. I used always try to say, 'That's me. That's the real me. I am not the great fellow I might be tempted to think I am.' But that did not ease my hurt. I'd have a sinking feeling in the pit of my stomach. 'Oh no, not again!' I'd feel small and useless and humiliated and diminished. I'd feel hurt and despised as if I had nothing to offer. My energy would drain away. I'd freeze and go rigid. I seem to be fragile when it comes to my good name.

Eventually I'd calm down. After a long time I might be able to say, 'They may be right. I am like that. That is the real me.'

And at last I might even be able to accept it all as coming from God. From early on in this period of contemplation, I tried to reassure myself that everything that happens, though not sent by God, is allowed by him. And since it is allowed by him, in some way it must be for my good. Though, to tell you the truth, I could not see how these particular sufferings could possibly be for my good! I used try to say, 'If that is the way you want it, Lord, I accept.' Yet, I'd dread it happening again. And as regards getting over it completely, that usually took me ages.

Is that the purification?
Would I be correct in saying that those are the kind of purifications St John of the Cross was talking about? They are some of the incidents that stand out in my life. They might seem small to others, but to the person at the receiving end, they are humiliating. No glorious martyrdom here! Just a feeling of being useless and diminished.

Yet I often wonder, would those things have come anyway, whether I was trying to pray or not? I presume they would have appeared. However, I may have reacted to them differently. Perhaps one of them would have been the catalyst starting off the whole process of turning to God. On the other hand, perhaps I would have become even more angry. Perhaps I could have become a bitter person. I hope I haven't.

This period of purification is very painful because it is a two edged sword. Not only do our weaknesses and sensitivities have to be purified, but even our prayer is in need of purification. Indeed, I wonder if these sufferings were a preparation for this more penetrating purification, the purification of my prayer. I'll try to describe that in the next chapter.

CHAPTER 13

Our prayer has to be purified

One day a salesman for religious books came to Esker, our Redemptorist House in Co Galway. In his display there was a book I had not seen before. It was a new translation of the complete works of St John of the Cross by two Carmelites, Kavanagh and Rodriguez. I felt this should be more up to date than the Allison Peers I was using. I bought it and thus began a big adventure for me. I have already mentioned that, years earlier, when I was in Bangalore, I discovered a little book with extracts from John of the Cross by a Fr Stewart, SJ. That I carried around with me for years on my many journeys. Besides, I read many commentaries on the works of St John and St Teresa of Avila. But there were so many gaps in my understanding that I had not a clear overall picture of St John's doctrine. So here was my chance. I started off at the beginning of this big volume, at the first page of the *Ascent of Mount Carmel*. I did not read it. I studied it. I underlined the important sentences so that I could revise it quickly. I went through the whole book and became very familiar with some parts of it, especially sections of *The Ascent*, the *Dark Night,* the *Spiritual Canticle* and the *Living Flame.* Unfortunately, the volume was a paperback and from constant use it has broken into two pieces. Yet, tattered as it is, I'd be lost without my annotations and underlining.

I began to get a more comprehensive picture of the doctrine of John of the Cross. Though the language is very dry and theological, it is all very well worked out and logical. But I was in for many surprises. I thought the purification of our weaknesses, which I have just dealt with, was very painful. But then there was this other purification I had hardly averted to, the purification of our prayer. The need for this purification confuses many people. At this period, the way they are praying seems to be very good, certainly better than it was before. They think they are flying high. As I quoted John's words before, 'the sun of God is shining brightly on them'.

Dryness

But according to John all that brightness changes. John sees this as a turning point in the way they pray. One of the big milestones is reached.

Unexpectedly God allows a dryness to descend on them. They no longer get satisfaction from their prayers and good works. Indeed, these exercises become distasteful to them. The glory days seem to be over. They feel God has gone and probably forever. They begin to think it is their own fault. But why does God do this? They cannot understand why he should take away a form of prayer that is good.

However, John of the Cross has no doubt about the reason for this dryness. He tells us that God desires to lead them into a higher degree of divine love (DN 1, 8, 3). And that means he has to lead them from a base manner of loving and praying and bring them to a higher level. Discursive meditation and the prayer of simplicity are good but they are not an adequate means of close union with God. For now the aim is just that, closer union with God. It is no longer merely affections and insights that God wants. He is beginning to lead them into another way of praying.

It took me a long time to grasp what John of the Cross meant.

A new way of praying

William Johnston, in his book, *Silent Music*, p. 55, describes this very well. He writes, 'In the meditation of the great religions one makes progress by going beyond thought, beyond concepts, beyond images, beyond reasoning, thus entering a deeper state of consciousness or enhanced awareness that is characterised by profound silence.'

You may well ask, what in the name of heavens is this all about? There is mention here of meditation which is 'beyond reasoning' and 'beyond concepts and images'. He speaks of 'a deeper awareness and consciousness' of God and all this 'in profound silence'. However, these things are so intertwined that it is difficult to know where to begin explaining. So I will start off with the basic idea of knowing God.

Contemplation is knowing God and being conscious of him in a new and different way. This we must impress upon ourselves. But before we try to find out the new and different way of knowing God, let us have a look at the ordinary way of knowing anything. What is John's theory of knowledge? He followed the scholastic theory, which was current at the time. It is not all that difficult to understand, but it does require a little concentration.

The scholastic theory of knowledge

The scholastic philosophers held that we are born with no knowledge. As babies, our mind is a *tabula rasa,* a clean slate, an empty page. Gradually we begin to learn through the five senses of seeing, hearing, touching, smelling and tasting. I am sure we have all watched babies experimenting with all these senses. They put everything they lay their hands on into their mouths. They look, they smell. Their eyes open with wonder when they hear new sounds. In this way they gradually amass a lot of information.

And it was as babies that we, too, gathered all our knowledge. Then, by our intellect, which is the faculty of knowing, we analysed the information received by the senses. For example: we came to the conclusion that sugar, those white granules, tastes sweet; that some medicines have a bitter taste; that fire burns; that it hurts when I fall; that some music sounds lovely; that some flowers smell sweet and so on and on.

The intellect can also abstract, or draw out, from all these facts and arrive at conclusions and principles. For example, we can conclude that every twenty-four hours we have day and night. Eventually we realise that there are four seasons. If we throw a ball into the air it will always fall to the ground. Besides, we can have intuitions that lead us beyond what the intellect can reason to. For example, it seemed as if the sun goes around the earth, rising in the east and sinking in the west. But then one day someone said, 'Really it is the earth that goes around the sun.' A whole new bit of knowledge. In this way we are constantly building up a great store of knowledge. But it is all built on what we learn through the five senses. So all our knowledge is called 'sense knowledge'.

God is beyond sense knowledge
Now, because God is a spirit we cannot know him by our senses. We cannot see, touch, smell, feel or hear God. He is beyond sense knowledge. He is outside our ken. True we can learn things 'about' God through our senses. By looking at the skies and the world around us we can learn a lot about the kind of being he must be. We conclude that someone must have created the whole universe. We can judge that he must be intelligent and powerful. And that someone we call God. (Unless, of course, we are atheists.) So we can learn things 'about' God through his works. But to know himself directly, that is impossible for us!

To bring out this point, John gives us the example of a man born blind. He has never seen the colours red, green, blue, etc. He has no idea what they are like. No matter how much a teacher tries to explain, colour is beyond his experience. But he can learn the names red, green, blue, etc. He can even use these words. Obviously he gives his own meaning to them. But he still has no idea what colour is really like.

I remember meeting a good example of this. Some years ago, while giving a retreat, one of the sisters brought me over to the school for the blind. I met a young girl of about twelve years of age. She had been born blind. I asked her if she knew what colour her school uniform was. She was able to tell me the colour of her blouse, her cardigan, her skirt and her shoes. But when I asked her if she knew what these colours were like, she said she didn't.

Our knowledge of God
It is the same with our knowledge of God. He is beyond our powers of seeing and knowing and understanding, but we give him names. When we were young we heard about God, Father, Son, Holy Spirit, heaven, angels. Indeed, we are constantly using these words.

But we have no idea what they are really like, because we never experienced them. And because we have to think in images we formed some kind of image or picture of God, heaven and so on in our minds. These images we usually base on things and people we had seen and experienced. We might have thought of God as an old man with a beard, or the father of the Prodigal Son, or just brightness. It is the same with images of people like Jesus and Our Lady. Now, at a certain stage of prayer these images were not only helpful, but necessary, because, in fact, we could not think without some kind of image. Eventually these images became part of our reflection on the gospel and helped us build up a certain knowledge of God. And they probably led to feelings of devotion. Indeed, these images are what St John calls the remote means of union with God.

And now for a shock!

However, the images we have are false. They do not give us a true idea of what God is like. They are like the blind man's idea of colour. So John of the Cross tells us, logically, that these images, because they are inaccurate, will never be the *proximate* means of our knowing God, or of our being united with him. They are helpful only at the beginning as the *remote* means of getting some idea of God.

The implications of these images being inaccurate are far reaching. At a certain stage of prayer, they actually become an obstacle to our being united with God. And that stage comes when God leads us into contemplation. At this point, God is about to communicate in a completely new way. He will no longer communicate through images, words, ideas.

So if we keep going back to the old way, to those images and thoughts and words, we obstruct that new communication. The first lesson, then, that we have to learn from John of the Cross is that, in contemplation, these inaccurate images of God must go. They are in no way like God and are no help. Rather they are an obstacle. So out they go! However, it is not we who will get rid of them. It is God who will do so, because for us it is almost impossible to empty our minds of thoughts, words and images.

For example, let us try a little experiment: if just now you try to clear your mind completely of thoughts and images, you will find how difficult it is. All kinds of pictures and distractions will keep floating in.

But then a strange thing happens, when we are led into deep contemplation by God, there actually are no thoughts, no words, no images! All authorities sum it up in a formula that is easy to remember: in contemplation there are 'no thoughts, no words, no images'. In practice we now enter a completely different scene.

When God leads us into deep contemplation, we realise that thoughts and words and images just will not come even if we try. This is so unusual that we know at once that this is outside our power. Indeed, this is where the Holy Spirit comes into our prayer.

I know many intelligent people, who, when they hear that, say, 'That is impossible. After all we think in images!' They are right; for us it is impossible, but not for God.

But it still remains a puzzle for us. What is the advantage of having our minds cleared like this? The reason only gradually came to me. As I have said, God does this to make way for another kind of knowing which I will try to explain in a later chapter.

A painful process

And that process is upsetting. What a shock it is to go into pray and find our minds empty. We do not know what has happened to us when unexpectedly thoughts, words and images just will not come, try as we will. And this is something absolutely foreign to us because it runs counter to the way we have been praying all our lives. So we are perplexed. John explains that this is a purification into which God leads us. He gives it a special name: the *First Dark Night*. As a matter of fact, this is the term he uses to describe, not just the purification of our weaknesses, but also the beginning steps in contemplative praying. So as God leads us into this new way of praying, he begins to remove the images we used formerly. As a result a dryness descends on us, when we try to pray. Two things cause this dryness.

a) We are lost without images

When we try to pray images will not come. Or if they do come they are incomprehensible. Or we cannot hold on to them. Of course, we feel lost without them. They were the bricks and stones of the spiritual edifice we built. And now they are being removed, stone by stone, like the Temple in Jerusalem. That is painful in itself because we had become used to praying in that way and came to enjoy those sense images.

It is like a change of diet. We were used to certain food and now we cannot get it. St Paul speaks of food for children and food for adults. Now we are no longer receiving the food for children. Instead we are being offered this new food for adults. St John of the Cross gives the example of the Jews in the desert who did not like the manna from heaven, because they craved after the fleshmeats and onions of Egypt. I had the same experience trying to get used to rice and curry when I first went to India. My mouth was burned and everything tasted different. Then I got to love it and I still do! So we, too, in prayer look back and sigh for the things of yore.

This is indeed a dryness, a purification. All the sparkle goes out of our prayer. The sun of God which was shining on us so brightly, has gone out. That is devastating when it first surprises us. And then when this goes on for some time we think God, who seemed to favour us, has left us and will never return. The beautiful honeymoon is over. And trying to accept this emptiness will be a big struggle for a long time. The dryness will come and go, even for years.

b) The new knowledge is too pure and delicate

There is a deeper reason for this dryness. The new awareness of God, the new knowledge of God, is being poured into our hearts. But it is so pure and delicate that our minds cannot grasp it. The sensory part of the soul is not capable of being aware of God in this new way, and, as John puts it, 'The mind remains deprived and empty'. The mind can make nothing of it and as a result it suffers. It takes a long time before we become accustomed to this new and more delicate way of seeing and praying.

The eyes of our intellect are weak

John uses another analogy. The owl is a night bird. It can see in the dark, but the light of the sun during the day is so strong that it blinds the owl. It is painful if the sun or any bright light shines on it. It is like our physical eyesight. If we try to look directly at the sun with the naked eye, it can cause pain and we are blinded for some time. Our eyes are not strong enough.

It is the same with our looking at God. Our intellect is not strong enough to know him. It cannot grasp the wisdom of God. The reason for this is clear. We are capable only of sense knowledge.

So when God leads us into contemplation he shines this new light into our souls. It is so bright and delicate that it blinds us and we can see nothing. The result is we are left in darkness. Indeed, St John talks of the *darkness* of contemplation. God is darkness to us and the pain can be excruciating. However, gradually we become accustomed to this new delicate knowledge and the darkness that accompanies it. In time we will have a new awareness of God.

The God who is beyond us

When I first began to get some idea of what John was talking about, I knew I was being brought into a mystery, a new and different world I had not known before. God is not just another being, like all the beings or things we see around us. Nor is he merely a more marvellous and glorious being. He is in a completely different category. We cannot know him as we know other people and things. If we are to know him at all, it will have to be with a new and different kind of knowledge. I will now try to explain what this new knowledge is in the following chapters.

CHAPTER 14

A general loving knowledge

I said that in contemplation, we receive knowledge, but it is a different kind of knowledge. It is no longer sense knowledge, that comes through thoughts, words or images. Ordinarily we think in images, for example if I say to you, 'motor car', or 'tree', or 'home' the image of these will come into your mind. And yet this statement, 'no thoughts, no words, no images' is essential to contemplation as it is presented by John of the Cross, Teresa of Avila, the *Cloud* and most writers of what I would call classical contemplation.

A general loving knowledge
St John of the Cross sums this up in an expression that took me a long time to understand. He speaks of a 'general, loving knowledge'. And to explain it further he contrasts it with 'a particular loving knowledge'. I was meeting these two phrases frequently when studying the *Ascent of Mount Carmel*, John's first book. At the beginning the phrases did not strike me as having any deep significance. However, I eventually realised that they must have a special meaning since John uses them so often. It was only years later I tumbled to it, and then I saw their importance.

For St John this 'general, loving knowledge' is the real mark of contemplation, just as being *absorbed* is the real mark of contemplation for St Teresa. When eventually I grasped the significance, it seemed a simple idea. I remember the incident that helped me understand the two phrases.

The doctrine of St John of the Cross
It happened about that time that I was doing a course on spiritual direction in Manresa House, Dublin. Part of the course was to write

a paper on some aspect of spirituality. I decided to do it on the doctrine of St John of the Cross. I felt this would force me to study his writings more deeply. I think I had, by then, already read most of his collected works. But I got down to studying him more carefully. One night at about two in the morning, I was struggling with the meaning of 'a general, loving knowledge'. It did not make sense to me. Then I realised that John, being a good Thomist, always defines his terms. I tried to track down his definitions. At last I found them in the tenth chapter of the second book of the *Ascent of Mount Carmel*. I went through his distinctions and definitions and the meaning became clear. I now look back on that discovery as a great breakthrough. It was then I realised why John was making such a big distinction between a *particular knowledge* and a *general loving knowledge*.

In describing different kinds of knowledge, John distinguishes a knowledge that is both supernatural and spiritual. This he divides into two kinds: 1) distinct and particular knowledge, 2) vague, dark and general knowledge.

A particular knowledge
Perhaps examples would be a good way to describe a particular knowledge. Let us suppose I am meditating on the gospels and the picture of a scene comes into my mind. It could be the scene of the scourging at the pillar, or the traditional picture we have of Jesus with flowing robes and a beard. Perhaps a clear, defined picture comes into my mind. Or it could be an image we have of God as an old man with a beard. Or we could picture angels with human bodies and birds' wings in the way artists do. All of these would be like paintings or a film in the mind. They would often be clear and distinct.

Each of these John would call a *particular* knowledge. These images are all based on *sense* knowledge. They are based on things we have seen and heard. They are part of our human experience.

The general loving knowledge
On the other hand, the general loving knowledge is harder to describe. For John it is the opposite of the particular knowledge. In

it there is no particular or clear image. Rather, he says, it is vague, dark, obscure. There is nothing of our usual clear, human, sense knowledge in it. In fact it is so obscure that there is no image at all! So when we go into pray, if we have a clear picture or image in our minds, that would be a particular knowledge. If instead there is just a vague, obscure image, indeed no image at all, perhaps just a vague awareness of God's presence, that is a general loving knowledge.

A new kind of knowledge

However, while there may be no images in our mind there certainly is knowledge, a different kind of knowledge. In contemplation we go beyond sense knowledge. We do not see an image of God. We see nothing. We hear nothing. Yet we know something is present though what it is is not clear. Rather it is vague, obscure.

Does that mean it is blankness or darkness? Many, like John, talk about darkness. And yet it is not a 'dark' darkness. It is a bright darkness, if there is such a thing! Here we enter into paradox, or apparent contradictions. This darkness is called, in the old Latin tag, *clara caligo*, which means, literally, bright darkness. Again contemplation is often described as emptiness, yet it is an emptiness that is full. It is silence, yet St John writes of silent music.

Some of the great writers describe it as hidden knowledge and that is a good illustration. In contemplation we know instinctively that God is present, that he is near, that he is the most wonderful person there is, that he is power and beauty and majesty and intelligence. Now don't ask me how we know it. We just do. These attributes of God we sense in a vague obscure way. The experience is so enticing that we want to remain there in his presence. It is a hidden knowledge that does not come in words or images. It is knowledge in some other way. But what is that other way in which we get this general, loving knowledge?

How does this new knowledge come?

This is not the way we ordinarily know, yet there is knowledge there. How can we explain it? I doubt if anyone has given a full answer. All I can do here is make some suggestions from my own observations and from what others have said.

If I am in contemplation one thing I do know is that there is a heightened awareness of presence. I sense I am in the presence of something, though I do not know what it is. Yet it captivates me. Is God communicating with me through this heightened sense of awareness? Is it the Holy Spirit or Sacred Wisdom working within me? As St Paul says, 'But it was to us that God made known his secrets by means of his Spirit' (1 Cor 2:10).

What William Johnson has to say strikes me as being on the right track. He quotes St Thomas Aquinas as saying there are two ways of knowing. There is knowledge that comes through the use of reason. Then there is a knowledge that comes through 'connaturality' when one 'co-natures' with the object which is, so to speak, embodied in oneself (*Mystical Theology*, p. 50). This happens when we love and become one with the person loved. In prayer we love God and we become one with him. We have the same nature with him or, as St Thomas says, we co-nature with him. This is a knowledge that comes from the proximity of loving. It is 'a loving knowledge'.

Johnson quotes the first letter of John which emphasises this: 'God is love and whoever lives in love lives in union with God and God lives in union with him.' Thomas goes on to say, 'The lover is contained in the beloved in as much as the lover penetrates, so to speak, into the beloved' (p. 55).

This same idea is found in the vine and the branches, 'Whoever remains in me and I in him, will bear much fruit, for you can do nothing without me' (Jn 15:5). And St Paul uses different words to say the same thing: 'I live, now not I, but Christ lives in me' (Gal 2:20). We meet many uneducated people who are convinced of God's presence and love. Where did they learn that? As we say of faith, it is caught not taught.

Osmosis
So there we are, united with God and with Jesus in love. We are really 'in Christ Jesus' as I tried to describe earlier on. Somewhere or other, I do not know where, I saw the process described as being

like 'osmosis'. In general, osmosis means any gradual process of assimilation or absorption through the outer skin. The same thing happens if we pour water into a flower pot – the water seeps into the soil and from the soil into the roots of the plant and that, too, has been described as osmosis. If this is not too bodily an illustration, we are one with Christ and his life seeps into us. And his knowledge, too, seeps into us. We have this knowledge but we do not know where it comes from. It did not come from human learning, nor does it come through words and images. Rather it comes from our unity with Christ.

A loving knowledge too

But notice, John does not only say it is a general knowledge. It is something more. It is a general *loving* knowledge. Love comes into it. To explain this John talks of the will.

For him the will is the faculty by which we love. He tells us that there is given to the will 'a vague delight and love without distinct knowledge of the object loved'. So love is an essential part of contemplation. Obviously this is love of God.

When contemplation is at its best, we not only know that God is love. That could be mere theoretical knowledge. We know, with equal certainty, that he loves us. At times we feel a tremendous warmth and affection for God.

A summing up

That is a little glimpse of the theory behind contemplation. When we are led into it we are introduced to a new way of praying. We no longer meet God through words and thoughts and images. In contemplation, we meet God through a new awareness. However, we see him through a glass, darkly.

But to be able to meet him that way we have to be prepared. And God prepares us through purifications. We have to face up to our weaknesses, and God does this through the night of the senses, and it is very humiliating when he has to force us to see our faults. And then, our way of knowing God too has to be refined because the knowledge we receive is too delicate. So our very way of praying also has to be purified. Although this knowledge is dark and vague and obscure, it is a knowledge that brings greater joy and love than we have ever felt.

A step further
And now I want to go a step further and take a look at how contemplation works out in practice. From reading John of the Cross and St Teresa and other well known writers, and from listening to the experiences of other people and from my own experience, in the next section I have tried to pick out what I think are some of the main characteristics of contemplation. Though each person's way of praying is different, there seem to be things that are common to all. Some of these features I speak of you may have experienced, others you may not. You may have met them at a greater or lesser depth. You may have experienced things I do not even mention, or know about. And why is that? Because 'The Spirit breatheth where he will' (Jn 3:8). However, because you receive some of these gifts and do not receive others, does not mean that you are less or more holy than others. Holiness does not depend on greater or lesser gifts of contemplation. As I will indicate later on, the real test of our love of God is our willingness to be united to God's will and to do what he wants of us.

CHAPTER 15

Characteristics of Contemplation

People often ask what contemplation is like and how one prays in that state. So down the years I began noting down the things that seemed to characterise this form of prayer, both in the experience of others and in my own. I think describing these characteristics may encourage others. So I will go through them and perhaps an overall picture will begin to emerge. I choose my own order.

1st Characteristic: Stillness

For me stillness was the first thing I became aware of when led into contemplation. And it is one of the themes St Teresa has in her fourth mansion and that is the mansion through which we enter contemplation. But St Teresa has her own name for stillness. She calls it the 'Prayer of Quiet'. Indeed, I could not but notice this still-ness when it came into my prayer. It was so different from the still-ness I had experienced in the prayer of simplicity. I will try to describe it.

There is something deeper and more noticeable about this still-ness. It is a stillness that is more than silence or an absence of sound. I have been searching for words to describe it. I think the word 'hush' (which Carlo Caretto uses) gets nearest. You are struck by a hush that is almost tangible. It is almost a trembling expectation. It is like going from a noisy place into a room that has double glazing. There is a hush all around you. Eventually you begin to recognise it when it descends on you. Writers grope for other words the better to explain it. Though I may have mentioned them already, here are some of them:

* *Emptiness.* There is a sense of emptiness and yet it is not an empty emptiness! It is a full emptiness!

* *Darkness.* The *Cloud* tells us, 'For it is a darkness of unknowing that lies between you and your God' (CU, ch. 4, p. 53). St John of the Cross talks of 'a dark night'. There is a kind of darkness but that is too negative. There is nothing gloomy about this darkness. It is bright darkness.

* *The prayer of quiet.* This is the special name St Teresa has for this characteristic of contemplation. I have heard people describing getting into stillness as prayer of quiet. It may well be, in a sense, but not always, because St Teresa uses 'quiet' with a special technical meaning. For her it is the beginning of contemplation, and how she struggles to describe it! I think her best effort is in the 'four waters', in her autobiography.

St Teresa seems to have loved gardening. So, to describe the different stages of prayer, she takes the example of watering a garden. She tells us that you can water in four ways. The first way is by drawing the water from a well with a bucket. The second is by using a water wheel and aqueducts to guide the water along. But these first two ways are tedious and noisy. The third, if this is possible, is by having a river or a stream in the garden. Then there is a constant supply of water. The fourth is by rain falling on the garden. In the *Interior Castle,* she develops the third way, the idea of the spring being in the basin. The basin fills and the water overflows and there is no noise. She writes, 'The water comes from its own source which is God ... He produces this delight with the greatest peace and quiet and sweetness in the very interior part of ourselves' (IC 4, 2, 3- 5).

God does the work. We do not have to go through the labour and noise of meditation. It is all happening within us, in quiet and peace. The water just bubbles up from the source. I think this is a marvellous description of the stillness and quiet and presence that comes from deep within us. Is not that exactly what Jesus offered to the Samaritan woman at the well? 'The water that I will give him will become in him a spring which will provide him with life-giving water and give him eternal life' (Jn 4:14).

St John, in the third stanza of the *Living Flame,* goes on to say 'when a person is conscious of being placed in solitude and in the state of listening (by which he means contemplation)' he should remain in this solitude and inner idleness. Contemplation 'is always accompanied by a certain peaceful, tranquillity and interior absorption' (par 35).

* *The door tight shut.* I love this expression that Evelyn Underhill uses as it catches the hush I spoke of. This is what she says about stillness: 'As recollection becomes deeper, the self slides into a certain dim yet vivid consciousness of the Infinite. The door tight shut on the sensual world ... it rests quietly in this awareness: quite silent, utterly at peace' (p. 317). For me, 'the door tight shut' sums it up.

How to behave in stillness

And what should you do when you experience that stillness and inner idleness? Do nothing. Just remain that way. But to remain still is not as simple as it may seem. In the stillness many things will disturb you. All kinds of thoughts and distractions will come into your mind. Or you may feel you are wasting your time and that you should be doing something. You will be tempted to start imagining scenes from the gospel, or using words from scripture or bringing beautiful ideas into your mind. Don't. Stay still! In that hush there is deep prayer. But it takes time to accept that. Perhaps it is only when the other characteristics of contemplation are present that you will be at ease with this stillness.

St John of the Cross makes a point that has helped me. After all, he says, is it not an amazing thing that our minds, which are usually so active and full of pictures and ideas and distractions, can suddenly become so still? This is surely the work of God.

It took me a long time to accept that. I remember reading and rereading what St John of the Cross said. Like most of us, if I were in stillness, I thought I was wasting my time. Then I would get back to trying to do something. All to no avail until it eventually struck, 'But this is it! This stillness. This is what John is speaking about.' So if the stillness comes, just stay that way. You become used to it after some time and can be at ease with it.

2nd Characteristic: Joy and delight

Both Teresa and John of the Cross speak of the joy and delight one feels in contemplation. This joy comes when contemplation is at its best. Of course, there are times when it can be anything but joyful but at other times there is deep joy. I do not have the words to describe this, so I will let both St Teresa and St John do the talking.

St Teresa on joy and consolations

It is in the fourth mansion that Teresa begins speaking about contemplation. The first thing she writes about is the joy and consolation we experience in contemplation. It is obvious she has difficulty in getting the right words. She goes to great lengths to make a distinction that seems very important to her. She talks of *contentos* as being different from *gustos*. There are ordinary human 'consolations' which she calls *contentos*. These come from human situations such as meeting someone we love, succeeding in important business matters and so on. We can also feel these 'consolations' in ordinary vocal or discursive prayer. They are natural joys.

But she discovered in contemplation a completely different kind of delight and joy. These are 'spiritual delights' and her Spanish word for these is *gustos*. These are supernatural joy and delight. She says, 'These spiritual delights begin in God.' The *gustos* or spiritual delights are experienced in contemplation and only in contemplation. I suggest you read what she has to say about these in the fourth mansion, ch. 1.

St John on joy and delight

St John of the Cross speaks little enough about this joy in his prose writing. But he does say, 'This knowledge is more enjoyable than all other things, because without the soul's labour it affords peace, rest, savour and delight' (AMC 2, 13, 7). He speaks too of ineffable joy, that is joy that cannot be described.

However, it is different in his poetry. He lets himself go when he comes to talk of the sweetness of the embrace of love. A line that brings this out to me is in the 3rd stanza of the *Living Flame of Love*. He writes of 'the deep caverns of feeling'. As usual he gives his own prose explanation (par 18). But the line sparks off in me an interpretation of my own which I will add to his.

The deep caverns of feeling

St John tells us that there are deep caverns of feeling within each of us. Usually they are full of the dross of our everyday worries. These preoccupy us. However, we experience these deep caverns in a different way when the Lord empties them of this dross by his purifications. We have a terrible sense of emptiness. We realise how many nooks and crannies there are and all are now empty. This is real desolation, what one experiences in the dark night. But imagine the opposite, when a supernatural delight and joy rush into the empty caverns. You can feel it seeping into every crevice. Gradually it reaches every part and there is a sense of fullness. For me fullness has a deep significance. Humanly speaking what could be more satisfying than sitting on the shore as the sun is about to set on a beautiful summer's evening and looking out to sea. And if the tide is full, that completes it for me. This is a sense of human fullness and completion at its best.

Yet this is only a shadow of the feeling that comes when the nooks and crannies of the deep caverns of feeling are full to overflowing with supernatural joy. These are the *gustos* of St Teresa. Those who have experienced them tell us it is not possible to put them into words. They are ineffable.

Yet John is such a spoil sport! He constantly warns us of the danger of praying in order to get this joy and delight. We should rather go to prayer in order to be more closely united to the will of God, even if it means desolation. So I would advise you to enjoy the sweetness when it comes! John suggests that although we would love to experience these joys, we should not seek after them. But this is easier said than done. Once we have tasted them, we keep hoping they will come again in our prayer. And they may, from time to time, though often it is the opposite.

3rd Characteristic: Absorption

Now we come to what is the really important sign of contemplation for St Teresa. It is what she calls being absorbed. Just as for St John of the Cross the important sign was 'the general loving knowledge', so for Teresa it is this absorption. When you are absorbed, then you are in contemplation. Indeed, if examined, there is a similarity between the two ideas.

What does she mean by being absorbed? Let me try to describe it. You go to pray. As the period of prayer goes on there is a feeling of being gripped and held by an unknown force. You are quite content to stay that way. At the same time you are aware of the sounds and movement around you. Yet you do not quite know what you are absorbed in. It reminds me of the cry of St Peter, 'Lord it is good for us to be here.' Teresa sees this being absorbed as something that develops. At the beginning, she says, it may last only a very short time, perhaps the length of a *Pater Noster*. But then it becomes stronger and lasts longer as one becomes more accustomed to it.

St Teresa makes many attempts to describe this 'being absorbed'. She writes, 'The faculties are not united but absorbed and looking as though in wonder at what they see' (IC 4, 2, 6). In this state there would be few enough distractions.

Searching for words

And once again we find her groping for words. This absorption, 'does not come when we want it but when God wants to grant us this favour'. So it is God who leads us into absorption. Teresa has no doubt about that. 'If his majesty has not begun to absorb us, I cannot understand how the mind can be stopped', that is, how the thoughts, the images, the words have stopped (IC 4, 3, 3-4).

'When his majesty desires the intellect to stop, he occupies it in another way and gives it a light so far above what we can attain that it remains absorbed' (IC 4, 3, 6). Is this connaturality or osmosis?

However, we need a great deal of reassurance in this state. As Teresa says, 'Even if the experience ... is abundant the soul remains doubtful' (IC 5, 1, 5). We ask ourselves, 'Was the experience from God or have we imagined it or have we been asleep? We are left with a thousand suspicions.' It is good to have a director or confessor who understands what you are going through.

Being absorbed is delightful because it is linked up with the joy I spoke of. You find yourself caught and held and completely captivated. There seems to be something there that fascinates you and enthralls you. You do not know what it is nor could you describe it.

I have experienced this being absorbed very often. I find myself gripped and held. I want to remain that way. Besides it would not be all that easy to leave it. When the joy I spoke of is there too, it is, as John says, delightful. I would not mind remaining like that for ever. I wonder if that is what heaven will be like! But then the absorption gradually fades out and releases you. Now while this has been delightful, I would like to remind you again that there is the other side of contemplation – the painful side, the purification.

Could this be compared to being caught up in an engrossing book or being caught up in a spellbinding film? Or could I compare it to experiencing the catharsis in a play of which I spoke earlier? I suppose in a way, yes, yet there is really no comparison between the intensity of contemplation and any of these. I think rather it is like being in love. This is the imagery John uses. The model for him is the lover in the Song of Songs. One is yearning for the loved one. One wants to remain with the beloved. And this is what deep prayer and contemplation is about, love for God. Human love might give us some little glimpse of what loving God is like.

It comes in waves

Years ago when I was talking to the Brother in Calcutta he made a comparison that I could not understand at the time. He talked of prayer coming in waves. Years later I got a glimpse of what he may have meant. I often found that when the contemplation was very deep I was completely absorbed. Of course, I was conscious of what was going on and where I was. I was aware of the delight and wanted to stay that way. Then somehow, the intensity would lessen and I would, as it were, come to the surface. That would last only a few seconds and then I would be immersed again. That could go on, coming in waves for a long time. How to explain this? I wonder if the following could be an explanation. Could it be that we can take only a limited amount of joy or sorrow at any one time? Could it be that when joy or sorrow gets too intense, an inner mechanism shuts it off?

An incident might illustrate this. A niece of mine, my brother's daughter called Frances, died very suddenly at twenty-five years of age. Her young husband was left with three small children. It was a great tragedy and I remember going home to be with my brother and sister-in-law and the family. Each day relations, neighbours, teachers, school companions were coming into the house. I could not but notice the distress of my sister-in-law, her mother. I remember a group of friends would arrive and she would, as was natural, burst into tears and sob and sob. She was heart broken. Then, amid sobs, she would relate the circumstances of Frances' death. Before long they would be talking about Frances and recalling incidents from the past. Then quite soon they would be laughing and joking at some memory. Then, after some time, another few mourners would arrive and it would be the same again. My sister-in-law would be in tears once more and then later there would be laughter. I think that is the way at every wake.

Let me develop my explanation. We can only take a certain amount of joy or sorrow at any one time. For example, people say I was sore from laughing and had to stop. Again if we could not filter out sorrow and got too much of it we would be depressed. Psychologically we have to curtail our sorrow and joy. Perhaps that is what happens even with the joy of contemplation. It cuts off like a thermostat. It comes and goes in waves.

However, I think this coming in waves happens even more so in what I will speak of next, that is oblivion.

4th Characteristic: Oblivion

Both St Teresa and St John go on to speak of an even fuller absorption that can take place as one becomes more habituated to this prayer. St Teresa calls this 'the sleep of the faculties', or 'the state of union'. St John refers to 'oblivion'. You will find these described in IC 5, 1 and in AMC 2, 14, 10.

This experience can come as a surprise to many people, even though they have frequently been absorbed. I think at first it takes one unawares. It certainly did me. As a result it is reassuring to hear what both St John of the Cross and St Teresa have to say about it.

In the second book of the *Ascent of Mount Carmel*, St John writes about the general, loving knowledge which I have tried to explain. Then he goes on to tell us that at certain times this general loving knowledge has this effect: 'Thus he will sometimes remain in deep oblivion and afterwards will not realise where he was, nor what occurred, nor how the time passed. As a result it can and does happen that an individual will spend many hours in this oblivion, yet upon returning to himself think that only a moment or no time at all has passed. The purity and simplicity of the knowledge is the cause of this oblivion' (AMC 2, 14, 10).

John goes on to explain that 'this forgetfulness occurs only when God abstracts the soul from the exercise of all the natural and spiritual faculties' (AMC 2, 14, 12).

The sleep of the faculties

St Teresa, too, speaks of this oblivion but she uses different words. She calls it the 'sleep of the faculties', or the 'state of union'. This is how she explains it: 'During the time that the union lasts the soul is left as though without its senses, for it has no power to think even if it wants to. In loving, if it does love, it doesn't understand how or what it is it loves or what it would want. In sum, it is like one who in every respect has died to the world so as to live completely in God. Thus the death is a delightful one, an uprooting from the soul of all the operations it can have while being in the body ... It seems the soul is so separated from the body that I don't even know if it has life enough to breathe' (IC 5, 1, 4).

St Teresa feels this is still not clear enough, so she adds, 'It seems to me you're still not satisfied, for you will think you can be mistaken and that these interior things are somewhat difficult to examine. ... I want to mention a clear sign by which you will be sure against error or doubts about whether the union is from God' (IC 5, 1, 7). 'Well, then, to return to the sign that I say is the true one ... For during the time of this union it neither sees, nor hears, nor understands, because the union is always short and seems to the soul even shorter

than it probably is. God so places himself in the interior of that soul
that when it returns to itself it can in no way doubt that it was in
God and God was in it. This truth remains with it so firmly that
even though years go by without God granting that favour again,
the soul can neither forget nor doubt that it was in God and God
was in it' (IC 5, 1, 9).

How common is Oblivion?

When you read all that you will probably wonder if ordinary people like us ever experience this. I used wonder about that too. But
let me assure you, they do, and not just a few people, but many. I
learned this clearly some years ago.

Sister Margaret Dargan, an enclosed Carmelite nun from the
United States, was invited to the Redemptorist Retreat House,
Esker, Co Galway. She came for two consecutive summers, to give
courses. The first was on St John of the Cross. The second summer it
was on St Teresa of Avila. I remember very clearly the day she
spoke about oblivion. She said, 'Put up your hands those who have
experienced this oblivion.' I cannot tell you just how many put up
their hands, but I was surprised to see it was a very big number. I
think it could have been over half of a group of more than forty.
That reassured me, because as St Teresa says, we can doubt if this
really happened. I, myself, had had a lot of doubts.

My own experience

I had been experiencing this oblivion from time to time, but I did
not know what it was. I wondered if I had fallen asleep at prayer
and I was embarrassed if others were present. However, I was pretty
sure I had not been asleep. One experience I remember very well.

I was giving a retreat to the Mercy Sisters in the Mater Hospital
in Dublin. I am sure none of the sisters even remembers the retreat!
During a retreat to religious, I always like to end each day with a
silent Holy Hour or half hour. I simply expose the Blessed
Sacrament, read a passage from scripture and invite the retreatants
to pray in stillness. Then I end with evening prayer or a simple
benediction. I usually tell them not to distract themselves by won-

dering about the time or looking at their watches. I assure them I will give a sign when the time comes. As the time approaches I glance at my watch to check up. One particular night I came to, only to discover that it was time, perhaps just a minute or so over. I almost missed it. I was somewhat embarrassed, lest the Sisters would think I had been asleep! Pride dies hard! But what set me thinking was this. I was absolutely certain I had not been asleep because I was in no way drowsy. And as the same thing had been happening before on other retreats, I knew there must be some other explanation. I had a nagging thought in my mind that I had read about this somewhere. Well, I finished the retreat late one night and went back to Marianella. I went to the bookcase in my room and there was the *Interior Castle*. I wondered was it there I had read it. Though I was tired, I took the book with me to bed. I soon found the passages I have quoted above from the fifth mansion. I understood what Teresa was talking about because that was the same experience as I had had. And there had been the very same doubts she wrote about. Had I been asleep? Or was I awake? And yet I knew that on that particular night, and on other nights too, I had not been asleep.

According to John, this oblivion comes at an early stage of prayer. So it is not necessarily a sign that one has advanced very far.

5th Characteristic: No thoughts, no words, no images

I spoke of this earlier and came to a disturbing conclusion. The images we have of God and Jesus are not true images. They may indeed be what St John calls the remote means of our coming closer to God. But in no way are they a proximate means of union with God. John goes even further and tells us that, in contemplation, they are an obstacle to union with God. So we have to allow God to empty our minds of these until eventually we are left with the vague, obscure, dark, general knowledge. Then there is some possibility of our prayer being a proximate means of union with God (AMC 2, 10, 3-4), (AMC 2, 12-14). Let us hear what John and Teresa and the *Cloud* and Poulain have to say about this.

John's third sign

St John sums it all up in his well known third sign for leaving meditation and entering contemplation. 'The third and the surest sign' of
contemplation 'is that a person likes to remain alone in loving
awareness of God, without particular considerations, in interior
peace and quiet and repose, and without the acts and exercises ... of
the intellect, memory or will; and that he prefers to remain only in
the general, loving awareness and knowledge we mentioned, without any particular knowledge or understanding' (AMC 2, 13, 4).

How does all this work out in practice? Let me try to describe, in
so far as anyone can, what happens when one is in contemplation.
Let us suppose you want to spend some time at prayer. You might
try to create a prayerful atmosphere by thinking of God or Jesus or
scenes from the gospel. But gradually you notice that these images
will no longer come into your mind. Try as you will they will not
stay. Nor will words or mantras do any good. There seems to be
nothing there. No thoughts, no words, no images. At first I used be
very frustrated. All I myself seemed to be able to achieve was a
vague obscure sense of God being present.

Lo and behold, it began to dawn on me that this is it. This is contemplation. This is the general loving knowledge. It is dark, vague,
obscure. There are no words, thoughts or images. And yet there is
something present. According to St John of the Cross this is the kind
of knowledge we get in contemplation.

St Teresa's prayer of quiet

St Teresa of Avila has her own terminology. As I said before she
talks of the prayer of quiet. She also refers to the sleep of the faculties, or the suspension of the faculties, discussed in the previous
section. These are different words for what John calls the general
loving knowledge. For St Teresa, the intellect, the will, the imagination, the memory cease to function. In other words there are no
thoughts, no words, no images. And she tells us how we should act
on these occasions: 'Therefore in these times of quietude, let the
soul remain in its repose; let them put their learning to one side ...
Here there is no demand for reasoning' (Life, 15, 8).

The Cloud rejects all clear images

The Cloud of Unknowing talks of the same thing in even stronger terms. 'So then you must reject all clear conceptualisations, when ever they arise, as they inevitably will, during the blind work of contemplative love. If you do not conquer them they will surely conquer you. For when you most desire to be alone with God, they will slip into your mind with such stealth that only constant vigilance will detect them. ... Therefore, firmly reject all clear ideas however pious or delightful' (*The Cloud of Unknowing*, translated by William Johnston, ch. 9, p. 60). The *Cloud* does not compromise in any way. No matter how holy or pious the thoughts may be, out of your mind they must go!

Poulain speaks of the ligature

I remember years ago getting great help from what Poulain had to say about the 'ligature'. This word was used by the French Bishop Bossuet. It comes from surgery and means tying up a bleeding artery or wound. Here it refers to the tying up of the faculties during deep prayer. Poulain describes it in the fourteenth chapter of his book, p. 178. He tells us that an unusual thing happens in deep prayer. At times, you find that you cannot use images or words. Poulain describes this. While in the stillness of contemplation you might say to yourself, 'I am wasting my time. I must do something'. Then you try to say words, let us take, for example, the Our Father. You start, 'Our Father ... Who art in Heaven ... Hallowed be thy name.' But somehow the words are incomprehensible. Try as you will, they do not make sense. And eventually you just give up.

I have found the same difficulty in trying to bring images into my mind. Let us say that when you are in prayer and again feel you are wasting your time, you try to think, for example, of Christ in the boat with the the disciples. Yet try as you will the image keeps fading out or it floats out of your vision. It reminds me of showing an image on the wall with a projector. When you turn the lens, the image goes out of focus. You can see nothing clearly. Like that, the image in your mind goes out of focus. Despite all efforts it is impossible to keep the image of Christ in your mind, or to see it clearly.

And so eventually you just give up and try to rest in stillness. This is the ligature, or the tying up of the faculties.

Yet the amazing thing is that immediately after the prayer, you could sit down and write a commentary on the petitions of the Our Father or write a vivid description of Jesus in the boat.

If you find this 'ligature' happening to you in prayer, do not think there is something wrong with you. Many have experienced this. I suppose it is God's way of making sure there are no thoughts, no words, no images. In contemplation let us follow the advice of St Teresa: 'Let the soul remain in its repose; let them put their learning to one side'.

6th Characteristic: The What!

I know that is a strange name to give this section and it will need some explanation. It is actually taken from a line in John of the Cross's *Spiritual Canticle*: 'And leave me dying of, ah, I-don't-know-what.'

If all the authorities tell me I must have no thoughts, no words, no images, what is it I experience in contemplation? It may be silence and darkness and emptiness, but it is not blankness. St John tells us that if there is just blankness we would be wasting our time. In that situation we should at least go back to meditation or to loving awareness, which is really his name for the prayer of simplicity.

While contemplation is not blankness, nor empty emptiness, it is knowledge, hidden knowledge. In other words there is something going on. What is it? John of the Cross is trying to describe that in the seventh stanza of the *Spiritual Canticle*:

'All who are free
Tell me a thousand graceful things of you;
All wound me more
And leave me dying
of, ah, I-don't-know-what behind their stammering.'

What John is saying is this: All the graceful things I learn of you, my God, wound me and leave me dying. Yet I do not understand and so I stammer like a child. I do not know what it is. It is a lofty understanding of God that cannot be put into words. Since it is not understandable, it is indescribable. It is 'I-don't-know-what'.

My own personal experience

When I look back on my prayer, I remember that I have so often entered it only to find great difficult in settling down. But then gradually everything calmed down. Peace and quiet descended. St Teresa describes it this way, 'One noticeably senses a gentle drawing inward ...(like) a hedgehog curling up or a turtle drawing into its shell' (IC 4, 3, 3-4).

However, there seemed to be something present that fascinated me. It was not something I brought to my mind or imagined, it was just there. There was no movement, all was still, I just looked at it. It mesmerised me and yet I had not a clue what it was. Whatever it was, it was the most enthralling thing I ever experienced. I just wanted to stay there in the presence of this, 'The What'. Usually I was fully aware all the time, knowing where I was.

And yet there was a timelessness about it. While it was happening, I did not know how long I had been there. However, while the prayer was going on, there was no sense of rush. Rather I was content to stay looking because I was enthralled.

Reflecting on my experience

There is a tendency in all of us to relive our experiences and analyse them. Indeed, it is in this reflection that we begin to understand in some way the meaning of what we have experienced. I think this is what T. S. Eliot is saying in the third of his *Four Quartets*:

We had the experience but missed the meaning,

And approach to the meaning restores the experience

In a different form (*The Dry Salvages*).

Often we experience things and miss the meaning of what took place. And so I have frequently found myself going back and analysing what happened in prayer and searching for meaning. John and Teresa obviously did the same thing!

I sat there looking back on the experience and found I could recreate it, up to a point. It was as if I were outside myself, like a third party, looking at myself in prayer. I could see myself gazing at that something that was before me. I knew that during the actual prayer I could see it only vaguely and obscurely and so I did not know what it was. But I did know for certain that while the prayer lasted, I had been enthralled and held.

So on reflection, I could recreate the scene, but the actual experience of being enthralled I could not recreate. If I could have, I would have been able to enter contemplation when I wanted. And that is not possible. As Eliot says, we can restore the experience in a different form. I could restore everything except the kernel, the being enthralled.

Otto's 'The Idea of the Holy'

I found a description of the same experience in *The Idea of the Holy*, by Rudolf Otto, the German theologian. Otto, too, tries to analyse this encounter we experience in deep prayer. He speaks of an 'unnamed something' that is part of religion. He says, 'There is no religion in which it (the unnamed something) does not live as the real innermost core' (p. 6). He searches for names to give it and comes up with three. He calls it 'The Holy', 'The Numinous', 'The Wholly Other'.

Otto then analyses his idea of the Holy. He defines 'The Holy' in his well know phrase: *mysterium tremendum et fascinans*, which can be translated as 'a terrible and fascinating mystery'. *Mysterium* is not just mystery in the sense of something unknown or unexplained. Here it is something that is beyond our comprehension. Our minds just cannot grasp it. It is wholly other. And yet, it fills our minds with wonder and astonishment.

This mystery, this something which we cannot understand, is *tremendum*. It has the element of daunting awfulness and majesty. But it is also *fascinans*, fascinating. There are these two opposites present at the same time. The person trembles before it while at the same time he turns to it to make it his own. On the one hand, it bewilders and confounds. On the other hand, it captivates and transports him (p. 31).

When I read all that I realised that this was what I had been trying to say. But then Otto goes further. He gives a marvellous description of how this mystery, which is both awful and fascinating, can effect us. The details he gives are far more varied than I have ever experienced. So, I will give a number of his little word pictures, as some of them may speak to certain people better than I can.

He writes, 'This (the Numinous, the Holy) is felt as an Object outside oneself ... It grips and stirs the human mind, occupying it with a wellnigh bewildering strength ... The feeling of it may at times come sweeping like a gentle tide pervading the mind with a tranquil mood of deepest worship ... continuing as it were, thrillingly vibrant and resonant ... It may burst in sudden eruption up from the depths of the soul with spasms and convulsions, or lead to the strangest excitements, to intoxicated frenzy, to transport and to ecstasy ... It may develop into something beautiful and pure and glorious. It may become the hushed, trembling and speechless humility of the creature in the presence of – whom or what? In the presence of that which is a mystery inexpressible and above all creatures.'

The aftermath
For me, the after-effects of the experience of 'The What' were varied. Usually I came out of this prayer in a glow, carrying the sense of presence with me for hours. On the other hand, I remember telling my director at a retreat in Manresa House that there was so little aftermath that I might as well have been walking on Dollymount strand! But usually the presence lingered on. It seems to me that the closest human experience is falling in love. And indeed that is what is happening to us – it is an experience of love. We fall in love with God.

7th Characteristic: Contemplation is passive prayer
If you speak to contemplatives they will tell you that this prayer does not come from themselves. It is something that has been given to them, a gift. So it is not possible to bring on contemplation because this is *passive* prayer. It is the opposite of *active* prayer.

The word passive has, in general, two main meanings. First of all, you can say that someone is passive and mean that he is just there, doing nothing, unresisting. This is not the meaning we give it when talking about prayer.

Passive has another meaning. It means being affected by or acted on by someone or something else. Grammar may help us to understand this better. The *active voice* is when the subject does the action, for example, I strike, or I love or I pray. It is 'I' who am doing the striking, the loving, the praying. In the *passive voice*, I do not do the action, rather 'I suffer the action' or 'I am acted upon'. Examples of the passive voice are I am struck, I am loved. We could even coin a new word 'I am prayed'. I do not do the praying; rather, to use a clumsy phrase, the praying is done on me. This is exactly what we mean by passive prayer. It is not prayer that I do. Rather, God does the praying in me.

So, active prayer is the praying I do. I initiate it and continue it. Passive prayer is the prayer God or the Spirit does within me.

This is what St Paul seems to be talking about in Romans 8:26: 'For we do not know how we ought to pray: the Spirit himself pleads with God for us in groans that words cannot express'.

When we are led into contemplation, our prayer changes from active to passive prayer. Up until this we have been doing the praying. We started it and chose what way to continue. But in contemplation, which is passive prayer, we are carried into it. Indeed, it is the Spirit who now does the praying within us. It is a feeling of being taken over and being led in a way we could not go by ourselves.

Contemplation is a gift of God. St Teresa and St John were very conscious of this. What St Teresa had to say about being absorbed in prayer brings this out very clearly. 'If his majesty has not begun to absorb us, I do not understand how the mind can stop' (IC 4, 3, 4).

8th Characteristic: Simultaneity and succession

What got me thinking of this was a statement by Evelyn Underhill. She says, 'The natural mind is conscious only of succession: the special *differentia* of the mystic is the power of apprehending simultaneity' (p. 239). Evelyn is, of course, talking about ways of knowing and apprehending. She makes a distinction between two ways. Succession means that one thought follows another. Simultaneity means knowing everything at the same time.

Succession

This is the way we usually think. We grasp one part after another or one idea after another. It is like a novel unfolding. One thought, one scene, one chapter follows another until the whole story unfolds.

Do you remember geometry at school? When we had to prove a theorem of Euclid, we did it step by step. This side is equal to that side and this side is equal to that side. Therefore those two angles are equal. And we ended with Q.E.D., *quod est (erat) demonstrandum* – what was to be proved! That is thinking in succession.

Simultaneity

This is another way of knowing. To see everything at once. This is the knowledge of the creator. Does this explain how God sees the whole universe, the whole of creation at one glance? Does he see every person and thing at one glance? Does it also explain how he sees the whole of history from beginning to end?

The knowledge of the creature, our knowledge, is ordinarily successive knowledge. But in the intense concentration of contemplation do we get a little share in the simultaneity of God? I had this very much in mind when talking about 'The What' and 'being absorbed'. There is that deadly concentration on one thing. What we see is so simple and so much of a whole that we see it all at once. And we know afterwards that we have been concentrated and absorbed and held in looking at that one thing. There is something ecstatic about it.

Do we grasp simultaneously in contemplation?

Evelyn Underhill describes another facet of this. She quotes some-one as saying that pure contemplation is 'that state of deep orison in which the subject seems to be seeing, feeling and thinking all at once' (p. 243). In contemplation there is that terrible concentration on whatever is attracting one. 'By this spontaneous exercise of all his powers under the dominion of love, the mystic attains that vision of the heart.' Is it here we meet God, the ground of our being? Do we come close to 'Being', to 'Existence' itself. Is it here we get to the heart of the matter?

At prayer I am often struck by the oneness of everything. The whole universe is one. In the big bang, the one central element scattered and solidified into the whole universe and the stars and the planets and the earth and each one of us. I am fascinated by the thought that we are made of the same stuff as the stars. The whole universe is one and all of us in the universe are part of it. And we are all one in God who keeps us in existence. Often in prayer I am conscious of our oneness. Or again take the Father, Son and Holy Spirit, they are all united in one Trinity. Is receiving a vision of the Trinity in the seventh mansion part of this simultaneity? Does that deadly concentration of contemplation have to reach the heights before we in some way make sense of the oneness of the Trinity?

9th: Viewing all the characteristics together

People may already be in contemplation but do not realise it. If we were to take all these characteristics together and have a brief look at the whole scene, we might begin to see more clearly. I am sure each reader will be aware of some characteristics more than others and perhaps experience other characteristics I have not mentioned.

Following John, Teresa and our other teachers of classic contemplation, something like the following begins to appear:

We go into pray and gradually settle down. Then we notice the stillness and the hush. As the prayer goes on, the joy and peace increases. We see nothing or hear nothing. Into this silence comes the sense of being absorbed, held and gripped. We do not really know what is gripping us but we sense we are in the presence of something. Yet we are convinced that it is real. God is there. There are no words, no thoughts, no images. Indeed, words and images will not stay in our minds even if we try. Rather there is something general and vague and obscure. It is the general loving knowledge. It is so fascinating that we want to stay like this.

At the same time we are conscious that this is a gift of God. We could not achieve this on our own because this is not the way we know things normally. So, obviously God is intervening.

In this contemplation there may seem to be darkness and emptiness. But there is knowledge. How we get that knowledge, without thoughts and words and images, is difficult to explain. We just know that God is present and near us. We know we are in the presence of something, we know not what. Yet we know with certainty that it is the most beautiful thing imaginable. It is so enthralling that we want to remain in its presence. We know that it is God and that God is love and we do not doubt that he loves us and wants us. We long for this presence to go on and on.

If this gives the feel of contemplation, it is only the beginning. There is much more to follow and it may take years and years to be lead through all the stages. However, very few ever get that far. Much of these later stages are beyond me because I have not experienced them. So to describe them, I will have to depend a lot on John and Teresa and the other great contemplatives in the chapters that follow.

CHAPTER 16

The Second Dark Night

The next subject to discuss is the second dark night. I wondered how to approach it as I have little experience of it and have still a long way to go. So all I can do is tell you my own scanty experience and what I learned from St John of the Cross, St Teresa and others.

The phrase 'the dark night' conjures up the idea of the purification and agony we must go through as we advance in prayer. That is true in a sense, but John uses the phrase in a slightly different way. For him it is the whole process of going to God, not only the painful, dark purification but also the delightful prayer I have been describing. For John they are all one, just different aspects of the same journey.

You may remember that in the first dark night God purges us of our more obvious and superficial faults. This John calls the night of the senses. I have tried to describe that night in chapters 12 and 13 where both our weakness and our way of praying were purged. But then there is another and deeper purgation, the night of the spirit, which comes later. Here God wants to get at the root of our faults. For John it is like the difference between pulling the head off a weed and digging up the root. Or it is like the difference between rubbing out a fresh stain on a cloth as opposed to trying to wash out a deeply embedded stain.

St John on this dark night
'This dark night (the second) is an inflow of God into the soul, which purges it of its habitual ignorances and imperfections, natural and spiritual, and which contemplatives call infused contemplation or mystical theology ... God teaches the soul secretly and instructs it in the perfection of love without it doing anything nor understand-

ing how this happens. ... Contemplation prepares the soul for the union of God through love by both purging and illumining it' (DN 2, 5, 1).

Contemplation is a mixture of marvellous joy and tedium and intense pain. It is a series of ups and downs. St John of the Cross uses the name dark night to convey all that. So he can refer to it as a delightful night and a painful night. It is both. I remember when I used be fluctuating between the two extremes of joy and purgation an image often came into my mind. It was the image of a tropical island which may help to describe this period of prayer.

The tides on a tropical island
I used imagine the 'soul' as a tropical island, like one of those beautiful islands in the Pacific Ocean. There are the usual palm trees with a beautiful sandy beach sloping to the water's edge. Each day the tide comes in and goes out, there is low tide and high tide. The sea does not go out very far nor does it come in very far.

But each month, with the full moon and the new moon come the spring tides. Then the sea rises higher until it covers most of the island and only the trees appear. Eventually the sea ebbs and at low tide it goes out so far it can hardly be seen in the distance. After a few days the tides return to the ordinary daily ebb and flow.

That seemed to me a good example of the way contemplation ebbs and flows. Ordinarily, prayer and living go on calmly enough. The prayer is fairly peaceful and still, and even though it does not go very deep it is satisfying enough. At these times there are no big trials or sufferings. These are the ordinary tides. But then, all changes.

When the spring tides come the sea flows. Then the tide rushes in so far that it almost covers the whole island. It is as if the Lord has overwhelmed us. These are the times of being immersed in the prayer that I have described. We feel we are being embraced by God and the love of God rises in our hearts.

But then the tide goes out until we can scarcely see it. The Lord, too, ebbs and goes so far away we can scarcely sense his presence. Indeed, we may have no awareness of him at all. A feeling of desolation descends upon us. When we go to pray we cannot settle down or be still and peaceful. Our mind is agitated and running to other things. Or perhaps our mind seems heavy and we are unable to raise it in prayer. We seem to have lost all enthusiasm for God and prayer. Our prayer, which formerly seemed easy enough, now seems impossible. All our fervour has gone. Our savour for the things of God has evaporated. At times, if we are in the chapel, we can remain there no longer but have to get up and go. Even if we think we will stick it for some time longer, a strong compulsion drives us out.

And the worst of it is we feel it is all our own fault and that we have blown it. We have been so unfaithful that God has gone away and will never return. The beautiful honeymoon is over and we ourselves are the cause.

Then moments of doubt come when we feel that those glorious periods of prayer were an illusion. We cannot understand how they had at one time seemed so wonderful and now appear so drab and unattractive. There is a temptation to give up prayer altogether. I have gone through this so often that I know in this stage of prayer we need a lot of encouraging. (Thank God for an understanding director.)

Or it could be that there is some unexpected trial in our daily life. For instance, we have had a misunderstanding with someone and it disturbs us. Or some project we have been engaged in is not going well. Indeed, all our work may seem to be a down right failure. Or our health is not good. Or our friends seems to have abandoned us. We can get no help from books or spiritual directors. So many things are going wrong that there is a sense of emptiness and blackness. It seems like depression and, indeed, St John uses the word melancholia. Then we conclude that the time of consolation is over and will never return.

And yet we do not want it to go away because it is the most precious thing we have. We yearn for it to return, otherwise life would be empty and drab. We would do anything to get it back, even if it meant more suffering. If we thought that suffering were the sign that God is returning, we'd welcome it gladly. We promise that we will try to be more faithful at prayer and at loving God. We will cut out those sins and unfaithfulness from our life for they may well be the cause of God abandoning us.

However, the analogy with the tides does not hold in every detail. The spring tide goes far, far out but only for a short time. After a few days all will be back to normal. But when this period of purgation comes, the absence of God and the inability to pray can go on for a long time. Indeed, God can be absent for so long that we feel the purgation will never end.

God returns

Then God returns. It is as if God has overwhelmed us again and once more embraced us. We are saturated with God. We find we can pray once more. We feel like the Jews returning from Babylon when their mouths were filled with laughter. The winter is past. John of the Cross says we feel the purgation has gone for ever and will never come again.

These seem to be the usual high points and low points in contemplation. St John of the Cross describes all this in DN 2, 5-10.

Why this suffering?

St John goes on to tell us that this affliction and torment comes about for two reasons.

1) The height of the divine wisdom which exceeds the capacity of the soul. He puts it this way: 'This divine light is so bright that it overwhelms the intellect and deprives it of its natural vigour. It is a ray of darkness for the soul' (DN 2, 5, 2-3).

2) The second cause is the soul's baseness and impurity. The soul has still so many faults that it is not yet ready to receive this divine wisdom. The dark night makes the soul so aware of this that the agony comes. 'Then the soul is convinced that God has rejected it and with abhorrence cast it into darkness. He feels he is forsaken and despised particularly by his friends' (DN 2, 6, 2-3).

St John says, 'The soul feels too these evils will never end. It can find neither consolation nor support in any doctrine or spiritual director. He feels they do not understand him. These sufferings will go on for many years' (DN 2, 7, 3).

Consolation

But there is relief as when the spring tide almost covers the island. St John talks about these intervals. 'But then there can be intervals when this dark contemplation ceases to assail the soul in a purgative mode and shines upon it illuminatively and lovingly. Then the soul, as if released from a dungeon, can enjoy freedom and peace and the loving friendship of God. Sometimes this is so intense that it seems to the soul that its trials are over' (DN 2, 7, 4). It is strange how we can convince ourselves of what we would love to hear! Formerly the soul thought the sufferings would never end. Now in the bliss of consolation it forgets about the suffering and thinks the present relief will go on for ever.

However, St John gives a warning. 'Yet when a person feels safest ... the purgation returns to engulf him in another degree more severe and dark than the former. And this lasts for another period of time. He thereby believes that his blessings are gone for ever' (DN 2, 7, 6).

That is John's way of describing the ebb and flow of the spring tides in contemplation. Though John says we think at times that the suffering is over, I must admit that has not been my experience! I am always expecting it to come again!

The in-between times

I have been describing the ups and the downs, the high points and the low points. But then there are the in-between times when prayer goes on quietly and calmly enough. There are none of the extremes of agony and ecstasy. This is the time of the ordinary tides. Though even then there are periods when it is a struggle just trying to settle down to stillness in prayer. Often the stillness will not come. But you just keep on going!

St John tells us all this should lead to union with God. To me that sounded at first beautiful and consoling, but it turned out to be more difficult than I had imagined. I will look at the path to union with God in the next chapter.

CHAPTER 18

What is union with God?

I have always thought that was a wonderful aim to have in life – to be united with God. After all, that is the aim of Christianity and of the religious life. For me, I suppose that realisation goes back to my seminary days when there was great emphasis on becoming one with Christ, like in the union of the vine and the branches. One of the books I think we all read at that time was *Christ the Life of the Soul*, by the Abbot Marmion. Even the very title sums up what Christianity is about.

So when I started studying John more carefully, I was pleased to discover early on, in the second book of the *Ascent*, that he has a chapter called 'explanation of the nature of union with God'. I said to myself, 'This is what I am looking for.'

Faith

But then I ran into a mental block because I could not see a straight line in his argument. He starts off with one of his basic principles, that faith is the proximate means of union with God. That I have no difficulty in accepting. But then he defines faith as 'an obscure habit because it brings us to believe divinely revealed truths which transcend ... all human understanding' (AMC 2, 3, 1).

This definition was my problem. I took revealed truths to mean things like the articles of the creed we recite on Sundays at Mass. Now that seemed to be a purely intellectual acceptance. Prayer, on the other hand, had to do with a relationship with God. I could not fit the two together.

Some years ago I found a solution when writing about faith. I asked myself what faith in the Bible meant. What I discovered seemed to be the answer.

Faith in scripture

When people came to Jesus seeking miracles, there was one question he asked, 'Do you believe?' He was not saying, do you believe in a list of revealed truths. Rather he was saying, 'Do you believe I have the power to do this? Do you believe I want to do it? Do you believe I will do it? In a word, do you have confidence in me? Do you trust me?' That's the kind of faith Jesus was demanding. And so it could be described as utter and complete trust in God and in Jesus.

Of course, this faith and trust does not apply only to the miracles of Jesus. It is bigger than that. It is a general attitude to God which says, 'I trust you, Lord, in everything.'

It is the same in other parts of the Bible. Take the story of Abraham in the Book of Genesis. God told Abraham to leave Ur and that he would give him the promised land. He believed and went. Then God told him that his barren wife would conceive a son and he believed. But then God told him to sacrifice his only son, Isaac, from whom his descendants would come, and he trusted God and prepared to kill the boy. St Paul praises the marvellous faith of Abraham. But that faith had to do with a relationship with God. Many scholars say faith could be better described as trust. So not only did Abraham believe, but he trusted this God who made impossible demands.

John on union with God

That is exactly what John of the Cross is talking about when he writes of faith. Faith is the means of union with God. This union with God comes about in my relationship with God. There is union between God and myself when my trust in God becomes so deep that my will and the will of God are in complete conformity with each other. In other words the best sign of my union with God is accepting to do his will in everything. Let us see how John comes to this conclusion.

John points out that we can be united to God in different ways:
1) Essential or Substantial Union
We are united with God in this way because he keeps us in existence. So every human being, indeed every thing in the universe,

has this union with God. However, this is not the union John is talking about here. There is another kind called:

2) The Union of Likeness

This union comes about when there is a certain likeness between God and the soul. That likeness is present when what God wills and what the soul wills are the same. Then John spells out this likeness in detail: 'This union exists when God's will and the soul's are in conformity, so that nothing in the one is repugnant to the other. When the soul completely rids itself of what is repugnant and unconformed to the divine will, it rests transformed to God through love' (AMC 2, 5, 3).

And from this there follows something else: the soul and God are not only alike in what they will, but they are bound by love. However, this is not just any kind of love. It must be an intense love. John refers to it as a vehement passion of divine love. This is what he says: 'The fruit of these dark straits is a vehement passion of divine love ... For this enkindling of love occurs in the spirit and through it the soul feels vividly and keenly that it is being wounded by a strong divine love, and it has a certain feeling and foretaste of God' (DN 2, 11, 1).

What kind of faith and trust?

So faith in God often down to accepting the will of God, in other words trusting him. It took a long time, but it gradually began to dawn on me, that this precisely is what God wants of me. I must trust him so completely that I will accept whatever he asks of me or allows to come my way. It is quite true that evil things come to us in life. We often refer to this as the mystery of evil. People are astonished and ask why God sends evil, especially to good men and women? In theory, I, personally, cannot imagine God sending evil. I look at it this way, if God is good, and I can see him as nothing else but good, he does not send these evil things. The only explanation that makes sense to me is that he allows them to come. Even this seems feeble.

But the practice is difficult. I must trust and accept that everything that happens to me comes from a good God. So it must ultimately be for my good. That takes a lot of acceptance because, for the life of me, I cannot see how certain things could possibly be for my good, for example, the humiliation after the Karachi mission. Yet when the chips are down this is the real test of my trust in God. This is the conclusion that John of the Cross came to. 'A person who has reached complete conformity ... of will has attained total supernatural union and transformation in God' (AMC 2, 5, 4).

It means just this: if even the darkest and blackest things happen to us, we say 'Yes, I accept.' Let me give you some examples.

How would we react if any of these things happened to us:

* If unexpectedly your husband or wife walked out on you;
* If the person dearest to you in the world were to die;
* If you were to get a stroke, lose your power of speech and be forced into a wheelchair for the rest of your life;
* If you were to see your sons and daughters making a mess of their lives while you were unable to stop them;
* If you had a breakdown and had to go into a mental home;
* If you were accused wrongly of child sex abuse;
* If you were to be an absolute failure and be mocked by others?

Now, all of these examples are real and happened to people I know personally. How would you feel if some of those crosses were to happen to you? What would your response be? I know what my reaction would be! I could not say yes willingly because the thought of those things terrifies me. Yet I would hope that I might ultimately get around to saying yes, even though reluctantly.

A loving trust

Any time I have ultimately accepted the hard things God sent me, it was only after a long bitter refusal and even then my acceptance was given very reluctantly. Yet that is not what John is talking about. A grudging faith like that could not lead to union. I feel that there must be still another element. The suffering must be accepted, as John of the Cross says, with love.

This deep faith, which is confidence and trust in God, must necessarily come from love or lead to it. And that love goes further, it leads us to desire everything that the loved one wants because we know that what God wants of us is for our good. Would that I could have unshakeable faith like that!

The burning log

What may help us to see the whole picture of union more clearly is the graphic comparison John makes. He compares the soul to a log of wood that is thrown on the fire. There are different stages it must go through before it becomes part of the fire.

When the log is first thrown on the fire it is green and full of sap. The wet and the sap have to be dried out of it and this is a slow process. While it is happening, black smoke comes out of the wood and before long the whole log is black and ugly. Bit by bit, the wet dries out and when the wood is dry enough the fire begins to enter into it. Gradually the wood starts to catch fire. Before long the whole log is on fire. Eventually, the log becomes the fire and it is no longer distinguishable from it (DN 2, 10, 1).

There is a twofold action going on at the same time in the log and in us. The purifications are like the sap being dried out of the log. Our selfish imperfections are being burned away until at last we can live in conformity with the will of God.

At the same time, the heat of prayer is gradually entering the drying wood. Our prayer is purified and, as the soul comes closer to Jesus, his life is seeping into it.

Each process must help and have an effect on the other. Closer to the will of God, closer to the life of Jesus, until at last we are transformed into God by love. I am constantly trying to make my own that prayer of St Alphonsus, 'Help me to love you always and then do with me what thou wilt.'

CHAPTER 18

The Vision Splendid

If it had not been for a couple of hours I spent recently in the chapel reading *The Spiritual Canticle*, this chapter might not have been written. I found myself in a situation I was in before. It was many years ago when I was still in Bangalore struggling with the prayer of simplicity. I was so anxious to know what contemplation was that I kept reading ahead in Lehodey and Poulain. I suppose I must have had some image in my mind as to what contemplation was like. But then, when I did eventually experience it, I realised that my image was in no way like the reality.

That's the situation I am in at the moment. For years I have been reading the 6th and 7th mansions and the later stanzas of the *Spiritual Canticle*. They create some kind of an image in my mind but I know it is no way like the reality which I have never experienced. So am I competent to write this last chapter?

It was at this point I took the *Spiritual Canticle* into the chapel and spent some hours reading those last stanzas. Down the years, I had studied the whole canticle, as was clear from the underlining and the copious notes. I understood the early stanzas in some way because I had experienced what John was talking about. But from stanza 13 on it meant little to me. But somehow on this occasion it moved me deeply. The poetry, the imagery, the love story seemed more full of meaning than ever before. That gave me courage. Though I have never experienced it, perhaps trying to share my limited understanding with you may help me and you too.

As in days of yore, I went back to Lehodey and Poulain who are good at giving a summary. Both of them present the development of contemplation under these headings: The Prayer of Simplicity (Mansion 3); The Prayer of Quiet (Mansion 4); The Union of All

Power or the Sleep of the Faculties (Mansion 5); Ecstatic Union (Mansion 6); Transforming Union (Mansion 7).

I have noticed that from Mansion 3 to 5, there is a continuity, one stage leading into the next. From the stillness of simplicity into the absorption of the prayer of quiet. Then into the sleep of the faculties when the absorption is deeper and lasts longer, often ending in oblivion. Perhaps it is along these lines that the ecstatic union, Mansion 6, will develop.

The 6th Mansion

And true enough we can see the continuity here, because St Teresa introduces a deeper absorption which she calls rapture. She tells us that rapture is like the prayer of quiet or the sleep of the faculties when it begins and at the end. There is an even deeper absorption and the senses do not function. However, it is during the rapture, in the centre, that something wonderful happens. God shares secrets with her (IC 6, 4, 3).

Teresa says, 'When the soul is in this suspension the Lord likes to show it some secrets, things about heaven … intellectual visions' (IC 6, 4, 4) Indeed, Teresa says that if the soul does not understand these secrets, the rapture is not from God but from human weakness.

And rapture is different in other ways. It comes on suddenly. There is not the gradual build-up as in the previous stages. It can come on even when one is not at prayer, or even when talking to someone. It is so overpowering that one cannot resist it. One is, as it were, carried along.

Besides, rapture has a radical effect on the body. Teresa says, 'He takes away the breath … the hands and body grow cold, so that the person does not seem to have any life … The extreme suspension lets up a little', and then it deepens again. It is like the coming in waves I spoke of (IC 6, 4, 13). The effects can last 'for a day and even days'.

Then she speaks of other types of rapture too, the Flight of the Spirit which she found frightening (IC 6, 5, 1), and the well-known Arrow of Love, which is sheer delectable torture (IC 6, 11, 2-4), but they are substantially the same.

In this mansion she speaks often of imaginative visions and intellectual visions, which, however, I do not understand.

From looking closely at all these stages of contemplation, a word Lehodey uses may sum them up. He speaks of 'ecstatic union'. It seems to me all the stages are some form of ecstasy, or being gripped and taken out of oneself. One stage leads to the next and the absorption goes deeper and deeper.

And then she writes of suffering so great that it reminds me of John's dark night. And it is about this time that the second dark night should come.

But even after these raptures and wonderful secrets, the soul is still not satisfied. It is longing for fulfillment, which is soon to come. The next mansion is a completely different kind of experience and the raptures usually cease.

The 7th Mansion – The Transforming Union

The new element in this mansion is the divine betrothal and nuptials. The soul is enflamed with love and yearns for union with the beloved. When men and women fall in love, it leads to getting engaged and then to marriage. This is the image Teresa develops. In the divine betrothals, as in human engagements, the soul and God are frequently separated. 'Let us say that the union is like the joining of two wax candles to such an extent that the flame coming from them is one ... But afterwards one candle can easily be separated from the other and there are two candles' (IC 7, 2, 4).

However, in the spiritual marriage their union and love is made permanent. This is the crowning gift of the beloved.

'The soul remains all the time in that centre with the Lord.' Just as when 'a tiny streamlet enters the sea, there is no way of separating the two waters (IC 7, 2, 4). This union is in the deepest centre of the soul. 'He who is joined to God becomes one spirit with him' (1 Cor 6:17). There is hardly any period of aridity or interior disturbance. The soul is in tranquillity (IC 7, 3, 10) and is now transformed into God in so far as this is possible in this life.

St Teresa speaks of an 'intellectual vision of the Trinity'. When not occupied otherwise, she rests in this companionship. But the presence of God is not always so clear, otherwise she could not live among men and women.

There are two effects that come from the spiritual nuptials.

1) The self forgetfulness she has been seeking all her life becomes complete because now she is always seeking the honour of God.

2) She feels a great desire to suffer (IC 7, 3, 2 & 4). As a result there is not lack of crosses but they do not unsettle her.

She regrets she cannot do more, especially when ill-health comes. Yet she assures us that God does not look at the magnitude of our deeds but at our love. The industry of Martha and the love of Mary must work together.

Souls in this state are no longer afraid of death. Sometimes they desire to escape from this exile. Yet they would be willing to live longer if in that way they could suffer more and give greater praise to God (IC 7, 3, 7). That echoes St Paul in Philippians 1:22. That is now her life, to love and to praise God who is her constant companion. I imagine that is how Teresa lived that last few years of her life.

I wonder if the spiritual marriage is like being constantly in the prayer of quiet or union, raised to the hundredth degree? And yet I know it must be something more than that.

John of the Cross on the Transforming Union

In the *Spiritual Canticle*, John gives a description of how the soul advances in prayer from the very beginning up to the spiritual marriage. It is his longest poem with 40 verses and a prose commentary on each verse. It is modelled on the Song of Songs and is more lyrical than his other writings. Like Teresa, John uses the stages of human love to outline the progress. He, too, talks of love and espousals and marriage.

It is in stanza 13 that John describes the raptures that lead to the espousals. And then the climax of the spiritual espousals and marriage begins with stanza 22. The soul has now come into the unitive way.

The Spiritual Marriage

John, like Teresa, describes how when a man and a woman are in love, they promise to give themselves to each other in the espousals. That is made permanent in marriage. It is the same with the soul and God.

St John puts it this way: 'This spiritual marriage is incomparably greater than the spiritual espousals for it is a total transformation in the Beloved in which each surrenders the entire possession of self to the other with a certain consummation of the union of love. The soul thereby becomes divine, becomes God by participation, in so far as is possible in this life ... It is the highest state attainable in this life' (Stanza 22:3).

Union

In this marriage the two are united and become one. I have already spoken of a union which comes about through a likeness of love in which the soul accepts, through love, the will of God in everything. But in the canticle he speaks of a different union: 'Just as in the consummation of carnal marriage there are two in one flesh, so also when the spiritual marriage between God and the soul is consummated, there are two natures in one spirit and love. This union resembles the union of the light of a star or a candle with the light of the sun, for what then sheds light is not the star or the candle, but the sun, which has absorbed the other lights into its own' (Cant 22, 3).

Transformation

And then something tremendous happens to the soul. She is transformed into God. You remember that John wrote of this in his comparison of the log of wood becoming one with the fire. However, his description here is more poetic: 'She has been transformed into her God ... For after the soul has been for some time the betrothed of the Son of God in gentle and complete love, God calls her and places her in his flowering garden to consummate the most joyful state of marriage with him. The union wrought between the two natures and the communication of the divine to the human in this state is such that even though neither change their being, both appear to be God. Yet in this life the union cannot be perfect, although it is beyond words and thought' (Cant 22, 4).

The Spiritual Marriage has taken place and then John describes other marvellous gifts that are given.

* Wonderful secrets are revealed. It is especially the mystery of his Incarnation that the Spouse reveals. John, unlike Teresa, does not speak of the Trinity.

'The bridegroom reveals his wonderful secrets to the soul, as to his faithful consort, with remarkable ease and frequency ... He communicates to her mainly sweet mysteries of his Incarnation and of the ways of the Redemption of mankind' (Cant 23, 1).

* Then his symbolism comes to the fore. There is the Touch of a Spark and the Inebriation of the Spiced Wine.

'This touch of a spark is a very subtle touch ... which enflames her in the fire of love, as if a hot spark was to leap from the fire and set her ablaze...Then the will is enkindled in loving, desiring, praising and thanking God.' (25, 3)

'The spiced wine is another much greater favour ... with which he inebriates them in the Holy Spirit ... It is more permanent and does not pass away as quickly as the spark. It usually lasts, even for days.' (25, 7).

* She is brought to the inner wine cellar. This inner wine cellar is the last and most intimate degree of love in which the soul can be placed in this life. And there are two effects (Cant 26, 3):

1) Forgetfulness or withdrawal from all worldly things.

'She takes little part in the affairs of others for she is not even mindful of her own.' And it is especially so with affairs 'that bring her no benefit' (Cant 26, 15).

2) Mortification of all her appetites and gratifications.

John points out: 'However spiritual a soul may be, there always remains, until she reaches this state of perfection, some little herd of appetites, satisfactions and other imperfections ... such as little possessions, judgements, eating, drinking, desiring the best. Some have more and others less of this herd ... In the inner wine cellar, all these are transformed in love, and they lose them entirely' (Cant 26, 18).

* She gives herself to him, keeping nothing back.

This is the most amazing of all. The way John explains this I find astonishing.

'She surrenders herself wholly to him. There is now no appetite for anything that is not entirely inclined towards God. She does not even suffer first movements contrary to God's will' (Cant 27, 7).

Now the reason that amazes me is that I always react automatically when God asks something difficult. Without my being able to do anything about it, there will be 'a first movement contrary to the will of God'. And not only a first movement, but many, many such movements! I am likely to keep on saying no. And if I say yes at all, it is a reluctant one! So this strikes me as a most amazing gift from God.

No wonder God gives the next gift!

* God communicates deep genuine love.

John speaks here of a deep, tender love.

'In this interior union God communicates himself with such genuine love that no mother's affection, in which she tenderly caresses her child, nor brother's love nor friendship is comparable to it' (Cant 27, 1).

One last sublime gift.

'Now she has not any other activity to engage her than to surrender to the delights and joys of intimate love of her bridegroom' (Cant 36, 1). Like lovers they look at each other. John describes that in a passage that impressed me when I first read it years ago. I will quote it all. I suggest reading it slowly.

Transformed in Your Beauty.
'That I may be so transformed in your beauty that we may be alike in beauty, and both behold ourselves in your beauty, possessing now your very beauty; this in such a way that each looking at the other may see in the other his own beauty, since both are your beauty alone, I being absorbed in your beauty; hence, I shall see you in your beauty, and you shall see me in your beauty, and I shall see myself in you in your beauty, and you shall see me in your beauty and you will see yourself in your beauty; that I may resemble you in your beauty and you resemble me in your beauty, and my beauty be your beauty and your beauty my beauty; wherefore I shall be you in your beauty, and you will be me in your beauty, because

your very beauty will be my beauty; and therefore we shall behold each other in your beauty' (Cant 36, 5).

In other words, the beauty and the life within us will be the beauty and the life of Jesus that we share.

You may remember when I was a student in Bangalore, I was very taken by St Paul's 'in Christ Jesus'. I made so bold as to suggest that we are really and literally 'in Christ Jesus' and are so united with him that we have no spiritual life of our own! There is only one spiritual life, I suggested, and it is the life of Jesus which we share in. Here John talks of there being only one beauty, that of Jesus, which we both share.

Indeed John goes on to say: 'This is the adoption of the sons of God' and he quotes St John's gospel: 'All my things are yours, and yours mine' (Jn 17:10).

What a mighty experience that must be in the interior of the contemplative's soul. And in *The Living Flame* John agrees: 'The experience of the spiritual marriage is so intense that if God had not favoured the flesh, by fortifying the sensory part with his right hand, as he did Moses in the rock ... nature would be torn apart and death would ensue since the lower part is unequipped to suffer so much and such a sublime fire of glory' (LF 1, 27).

In his commentary on the *Spiritual Canticle* he writes: 'The bride knows that now her will's desire is detached from all things and attached to her God in most intimate love' (Cant 40, 1).

The Canticle ends

'The bride sets all this perfection and preparedness before her Beloved, the Son of God, with the desire that he transfer her from the spiritual marriage, to which he desired to bring her in this Church Militant, to the glorious marriage of the Triumphant' (Cant 40, 7).

While I do not understand this stage of prayer, I sense that it must be a sublime state to be in, wrapped up in God in love, desiring nothing else. Human love fades into insignificance. I stand back in wonder that this is the height to which God could call us. God does, indeed, love the world and each of us so much. That is the vision splendid.

Well, that is the journey from our first stammered prayers as children up to the place where God has now led us. I feel, and I suppose we all do, that we will never get to the heights John and Teresa describe. And yet, after struggling with God for so long, I know that he is a God who never gives up. So we do not know what is in store for us.

All we can do, then, is leave ourselves in the hands of God and allow the Spirit to lead us to our destined stage. What worries me, however, is that I will once again become careless and lose whatever gifts the Lord has given me. St Teresa, too, had the same fear. She tells us that from the time she started deeper prayer she had the thought of the Rich Young Man before her. He was called, but had not the courage to give up what was asked of him. May the Lord give us the necessary courage to continue. I pray that he will lead each of us to the stage he has prepared for us.

Books consulted

Collected Works of St John of the Cross, Kavanagh and Rodrigues, ICS Publications, Washington DC, 1973.

Collected works of St Teresa of Avila, Kavanagh and Rodrigues, ICS Publications, Washington DC, 1976, 1980.

The Ways of Mental Prayer, Dom Vitalis Lehodey, OCR, Gill, Dublin, 1912.

The Graces of Interior Prayer, August Poulain SJ, Kegan Paul, London 1912.

Mystical Theology, William Johnston SJ, HarperCollins, London, 1995.

Silent Music, William Johnston SJ, Collins, Fount, 1977.

Being in Love, William Johnston SJ, Found, London, 1989.

The Mysticism of the Cloud of Unknowing, William Johnston, Anthony Clarke Books, 1975.

Revelations, Julian of Norwich.

The Holy, Rudolph Otto, Oxford University Press, 1973.

Mysticism, Evelyn Underhill, Dutton, New York, 1961.

Western Mysticism, Cuthbert Butler OSB, Arrow Books, London, 1960.